Embracing Difference

in a

Culture of Kindness

A Memoir of Our Time in Bali

Carla Newman Osgood, Ed.D.

UNITED WRITERS PRESS
ASHEVILLE, N.C.

United Writers Press
www.uwpnew.com

ISBN: 978-1-961813-78-6 (paperback)
ISBN: 978-1-961813-79-3 (ePub)

All images courtesy of the author.
Print edition produced in the USA.

To
Mom and Dad

Contents

Preface

I bow to the people of Bali who have created over this last millennium a culture of kindness which continually encouraged us to trust our curiosity and to listen deeply to all that arose from within and from without.

I am so grateful to my beloved husband, David, who held the vision, seeing clearly in his mind's eye how colleagues and students from two very different worlds could work together. From his vision this story unfolds.

The team. L-R: The author, Suryani, and David.

Introduction

The Way of Bali
Carla Newman Osgood

If I can listen to the mourning doves
And to the gamelan,

If I can taste sweet rambutan
And smell the sewage in the street,

If I can feel the language soft
Drift in and through my being,

If I can watch the Barong dance
To shower blessings on us all,

Then I can know the beauty here
And let it take me to that place

Where I will wait
For understanding when it comes.

Without the impeccable kindness of the Balinese people, none of us who traveled to Bali would have been able to embrace the differences we found. Their kindness flowed from a spring of consciousness embedded in their culture, inviting us to stay and explore.

Embracing Difference in a Culture of Kindness takes you into a time when, for over twenty-five years, my husband David and I traveled to Bali for a month or two. We left our clinical work as psychologists to be refreshed by the exploration of difference, an annual adventure which was as much a part of our lives as the seasons of the year.

This was a world in which the hot, steamy atmosphere of Bali danced with its people, their cosmology, and their sense of aesthetics. This dance lit up my reality, the prayer and ceremony of it imbuing me with a scent of the sacred. As I stepped into this dance, I became a part of it and was entranced, my mind and my writing taking on, at times, a dreamy, trance-like quality.

Dr. Cok Ahlit and Prof. Luh Ketut Suryani. The couple visited David and me in Vermont. Mt. Mansfield is in the background.

My story and the voices of our students are meant to leave you doggedly curious about moving toward that which you do not know. A word of warning: If you end up following your curiosity, you can expect to feel uncomfortable and vulnerable at times.

"Why would I do that?" you might ask.

Our students often talked about being out of their comfort zones, being confused, and not knowing what was going on. And yet, with humility, commitment, and curiosity, they allowed the Balinese people to lead them into a very different world. And, as the students did this, they learned more than they ever dreamed.

Many visitors in Bali felt a pull towards the unfamiliar. For example, I do not think my granddaughters would put riding elephants at the top of their list of fun things to do. Yet, while in Bali, they decided to try this. The mahouts sat in front of us just behind the two big ears of the elephant. As the elephants walked, the mahouts talked to the elephants, and they talked to us. My granddaughters, their mom and dad, and David and I listened. A relationship was forming that enabled us to feel safe and curious about the elephants that carried us. After the ride, my granddaughters approached the elephants slowly, touched the trunks of the elephants gently, and waited for a response.

The monkeys of Bali captivated my granddaughters in much the same way. And when we entered the forest where the monkeys lived, the caretaker talked to us quietly. As we observed from a distance, we came to understand that the monkeys were wild—not trapped in a zoo. They were free and moved in their environment as monkeys do, even with the presence of us humans. We were slightly frightened, but our curiosity took us into this new experience and kept us there.

Other visitors, however, did not want to listen to the caretaker, and to the reality that the monkey was in control. "Please do not look directly into the eyes of the monkey. The monkey may bite you," the caretaker advised.

A young woman, a member of a group moving through the forest, purposefully disregarded this warning, came forward, sat down next to the monkey, moved closer, and looked directly into the monkey's eyes. The monkey bit her fiercely on her face.

This rather dramatic incident was a good example of how, in meeting difference, it is important to accept help and guidance from others familiar with the terrain—in this case, the Balinese caretaker.

Accepting the state of "not knowing" was always at the heart of meeting difference in Bali. For example, to watch a Balinese woman in traditional dress standing before a tiny altar, holding her hand high, moving a blossom between her fingers through the swirling cloud of incense was to say yes to the stillness and to the mystery that enveloped her.

The author and her husband, Dr.David Osgood visit the Ubud palace.

During our second trip to Bali, a vision of bringing university students to the island started brewing in David's mind. He thought possibly our new friends, Professor Luh Ketut Suryani and Dr. Peter Wrycza, might be recruited to be part of the team. Academic standards had to be met, of course, but the most challenging task of all was to figure out how we could help students drop their self-consciousness about grades and achievement.

Peter Wrysza, Ph.D.

The course was designed for those working in the helping professions, to develop cultural awareness and intercultural communication skills. Peter recommended the title "Consciousness, Culture, and Community in Bali," setting the stage for us to adopt peripheral vision, something Mary Catherine Bateson often referred to in her writing, a vision that is holistic and illuminates the inter-connectedness of everything. The other big idea of the course was to approach difference with both cognitive and intuitive intelligence. For instance, when the Balinese healer was poking at the student's toe with a stick and it hurt like hell, the student was asked to trust the relationship he was forging with the healer and listen to what was happening within his own being, i.e., his feelings, the sensations in his body, the energetic actualities. In essence, the student was asked to hang in there, listen to his own experience, and wait for meaning to come.

We also asked our students to adopt an orientation towards learning much like that of the Balinese, one in which extended observation

Tjokorda Rai, traditional Balinese healer working with a student

took precedence over analysis and interpretation. When the students entered a new experience, we asked them to suspend questions for a while. When they could not understand the conversations that were going on around them, we asked them to rely more on their intuitive intelligence. Throughout the book, you will find descriptions of how the students did this, using their own experiences as their guide.

Dr. Cokorda Bagus Jaya Lesmana, "Yaya," his wife, Gusti Ayu Tesna, their children Cok Laksmi, Cok Gita, and Cok Bagus.

When the students settled in with families in the village of Tebesaya, they were met by a culture of kindness. This was a kindness not shallow, sentimental, and soft, but steadfast, saturated in strength, authenticity, and continuity. It was a kindness that flowed from the people, naturally enhancing curiosity and nudging visitors to open even more. This kindness supported when a student said, "I feel out of my comfort zone." This kindness said, "You are not alone. You are part of Tebesaya now. It is okay if you do not know. It is okay for you to listen to the sounds of the night, to hear the prayer bell ringing far away, and to feel the beating of your heart."

This book introduces you to an array of people—many Balinese and a few Westerners. What these people had in common was a desire to explore difference and create a community while doing so. As we shared our differences, there was excitement and confusion, laughter and tears, and always a passion to understand.

We welcome you now to join us as we take you into the world of Bali, as it existed not so long ago. To quote our friend Peter, "Take it easy. Take it as it comes!"

Part I

1
Currents

*The pilot's voice crackles. "Descent…33,000 feet…will…
airport…minutes…" I stir just enough to realize that I do not
know where I am. Something is gnawing at my ankles. I look
down to see my feet, puffy and sore, flopped out in front of me.*

*We are in an airplane. My husband and I have been flying
for thirty hours, stopping briefly in Frankfurt and Singapore. The
flight attendant looks right into my eyes.*

"What is she saying?" I wonder.

*I reach for the window shade, open it, and am hit with a blast
of sunlight. Beneath me lies a stunning expanse of blue. David, my
husband of twenty-seven years, and I are excited now, awake and
feeling the descent in every cell of our bodies. We land with a light
bump. The gigantic plane rolls along shaking ferociously, roaring
like a lion with a paw on fire, and comes to a stop. We have arrived
in Bali.*

*Currents in my life have brought me here. My mother died three
months ago; Dad died four years before her; our son Adam graduated
from high school and left for New York City to study art.*

I am in deeper waters now.

The young artist, Adam.

Adam survived high school with the help of his harmonica, his five best friends, and a couple of incredible teachers. He was playing music, painting, and sculpting with the same intensity that I was grieving. As much as he loved exploring the world of art and New York City, I loved being his mom.

But his childhood was over, and our parenting days were done. Society expects mothers to be delighted about this. I was not. Adam walked out the door, adrenaline pumping, fired up for the future. I walked out that same door saying goodbye to almost two decades of watching him dive into life, mastering one task after another naturally, seamlessly. When one task was mastered, he moved on to the next with even more energy and gusto.

"The best learners are children, not children segregated in schools but children at play, zestfully busy exploring their own homes, families, neighborhoods, and languages, conjuring up possible and impossible worlds of imagination."[1]

He was often drawn to the dragon's mouth, namely, to fire, excitement, and magic. He and his six-year-old buddies fashioned a world of their own. In the backyard, a cardboard fort took form, and all adults were banned from entry. About that same time, a handmade sign appeared on his bedroom door: "Do Not Disturb."

Life was happening. Adam was coming into his own. The cardboard fort disappeared. In its place, came a King Arthur-like tent with a banner flopping in the wind, which served as base camp for Adam and the rest of the knights. They plotted endless adventures along the bank of the river and in the forest beyond. These were the days of Camelot when imaginings and exploration took precedence over current affairs and schoolwork.

In middle school, Camelot was left behind, replaced by "adventures of the mind." Marathon sessions of "Dungeons and Dragons" were underway. As many as eight or ten of Adam's friends gathered in one of their bedrooms, spending the night together, and creating tales unknown to me to this very day. I suspect there was an abundance of savagery, triumph, and defeat in these tales, but I am not sure. The D&D sessions would last many hours and be repeated weekend after weekend.

With the onslaught of adolescence, however, the "bad boys" left their childish ways. With firecrackers, they blew up their childhood toys, i.e., their Star Wars figures, and Dungeons and Dragons sessions diminished, and the boys moved on to activities more likely to attract girls.

Around the time they all turned fifteen, they formed "The Illegitimate Blues Band" which later became "The Relics of an Unknown Legend" and ultimately "The Dirty River Blues Band." Each time the band changed its name, it became a tiny bit better.

But, always, the band was a magnificent "chick" magnet—or so they wished to think. On Friday nights, my husband and I would leave our 160-year-old farmhouse and go to the movies. We left these fellows, the solid six, to practice in the living-dining room. (What were we thinking?)

A fake early-American chandelier hanging from a chain above the dining room table was hoisted up and fastened to a hook screwed to the ceiling precisely for this purpose. The dining room table was folded to a third of its size and scooted to the side against the wall. Now there was space for a drum set and the drummer, Peter; a guitarist, Matt; a saxophone player, Corey; a vocalist & percussionist, Ish; the band artist, Tim; sometimes a bass player, Ben; and lead man, Adam, with his harmonica.

A large L-shaped couch facing the dining room (now the stage), provided excellent seating for what they hoped would be an audience of girls. The band continued "strumming their stuff" many Friday nights for the next three years. While their high school years were not the greatest for them, they had each other and, because of that, they knew who they were. Flare-ups occurred, but compromises, inspired by the urgency to keep the music flowing, came quite easily.

Remarkably, our home still stands, having held all of what was lived there by Adam and his buddies. A different kind of energy exists in this same space now. At times, however, I feel the vibes of the "Dirty River Blues Band" seeping through the walls, calling me to write about what I have learned from my family, my students, and my colleagues throughout the world.

While Adam was studying at Pratt, my father died. His death was caused by a rare heart disease that also took his father and brother in exactly the same way. The family was in shock. Dad had never been sick.

Mom and Dad engaged to be married, c. 1938

In the late seventies, Eastern Michigan University inducted him into their sports "Hall of Fame." In his youth, my father, Ferris Newman, excelled in track, football, baseball, boxing, and swimming. Standing six foot three, muscular and fit, he was often referred to as "the Rock."

As a child and throughout my life, I felt incredibly safe around Dad. He was a plastics engineer, a scientist, and an inventor. His proudest moment came when Dr. Michael De-Bakey, a heart surgeon and pioneer in developing procedures and devices for open heart surgery, consulted with him. Dad developed parts for the artificial heart-lung and artificial kidney, equipment used in open heart surgery and kidney dialysis. These very inventions were used on my mother when she had open heart surgery in the early eighties.

Some people, including his doctor, thought Dad was eccentric. I wondered what that word meant and why my parents laughed about this. My son thought Dad was a "gentle giant." At nineteen, he traveled from New York City to Mt. Morris, Michigan, to speak at his grandfather's funeral. Adam stood before his aunts, uncles, and cousins and said, "When I was a little boy, Grampa would whisk me up to his eye level so that I could look into his eyes. Then he really listened to me. He made me feel that what I had to say was important even though I was a kid..."

I had lost my father, and I was bereft.

It was up to me now to care for my mother, who was suffering from several illnesses. She had cardiovascular disease, arthritis, diabetes, cancer. My brother and I always thought she would die before my father but, in fact, she lived four more years after Dad's death. She seemed freer after Dad died, more fun to be with and curious about everything.

Because of her illnesses, she needed a battalion of people to tend to her needs. We arranged for her to move into an assisted care facility. She was unhappy about this—she wanted to stay with us. But our home was small. My husband and I were working full time. I knew that I could not do what she would like. Instead, we moved her into a community of older people, all of whom were struggling with various infirmities, some of whom became her friends. Mostly, she enjoyed the staff who came to need her almost as much as she needed them.

My mother was a natural therapist, a great listener, and remarkably intuitive. She counseled this tribe of caregivers regularly right up until the day she died. The staff wept and told me how much they would miss her. When I was trying to clear out her room, the staff lingered on. *Why didn't they leave?*

Then it occurred to me. Maybe they wanted something. My mother, Mary, had a collection of statues of the Blessed Virgin Mary (known as BVMs in Roman Catholic lingo). They were housed in a tall glass cabinet framed in honey-colored wood. The story was that my grandmother, Mame, identified my mom as the one of her five children who was to go to the convent and Mom had a short stay there. Family members, priests, and nuns, however, continued to give her statues of her namesake. I counted six BVMs in the cabinet. There were five staff members hanging on. Perfect! Each of her devoted caregivers walked away with a Madonna in hand, each looking as tranquil as the BVM they held.

The next day, I drove to the hardware store, grieving and angry, and bought two gallons of paint. My mother had had a painful death—one I felt she did not deserve. *Why did she have to suffer so?* She was such an incredibly kind person. My inner rant exploded into a two-day painting frenzy. I painted all four rooms of my office stark white. The dingy old rooms now looked fresh and clean. I imagined how pleased my mother would have been with my diligence.

I hoped that our trip to Bali might refresh our lives like the paint on the office walls. When the time came for us to leave for Bali, my rage was subsiding. *Would the rawness of my grief be soothed by the beauty of the tropics?*

Seconds before we landed, as I focused on the feeling of descent, fear and excitement arose. Peeping out the window, I saw a streak of orange-green, a blur of rooftops, and landscape. In that split second, I felt the presence of my mom and dad.

I was coming home, and they were coming with me.

2
A Second World

In 1991, David and I came across a documentary on PBS called "The Ring of Fire: An Indonesian Odyssey," filmed by Lawrence and Lorne Blair. This documentary was a twelve-year project, funded primarily by Ringo Starr and the BBC. Lawrence called himself a psychic anthropologist and did most of the writing. Lorne liked to be known as an adventure photographer. They were compelled to travel the unexplored islands of Indonesia, to travel farther and to dive deeper.

The episode entitled the "Dance of Warriors" explored the Indonesian island of Bali. Initially, the brothers were not interested in spending much time there because of its notoriety for being infested with tourists. They were more drawn to cultures untouched by western civilization. However, in a small boat, they sailed into a harbor on the coast of Bali, came ashore, and happened upon a ceremony.

In the beginning, it seemed the festivities were rather light-hearted, but then the brothers watched as things began to shift. Some of the Balinese were dropping into trance. Others stayed close by to keep everyone safe. What Lawrence and Lorne experienced that day, a ceremony called *Calonarang*, kept them curious about this culture for the rest of their lives. On another day, the brothers were drawn into a ceremonial procession which took them to a village, where the people invited them to stay. Lawrence and Lorne learned about Balinese cosmology and Balinese music, art, and dance by participating in the ceremonies and by living in the village. Their home, overlooking the rice fields, was built with the help of these kind people and for thirteen years was the place they returned in between their many travels. As Lawrence said in the documentary, "We found home."

Decades later, when my husband and I were taking university students to Bali, one of them wrote:

> "I think one of the most surprising things about the trip [to Bali] was the intense feeling of home in a town halfway across the world in a culture so different from ours..."[2]

Another noted:

> "Bali ceased to be just a place I was visiting. It became a place I was living, no matter for how short a time. Tebesaya became a home, and its people my family...But most of all, Bali no longer existed as a concept or a place to vacation... Bali was my home."[3]

David and I had found "home" in another country before we visited Bali. In 1966, among forty-five Peace Corps volunteers, we landed in Guyana, South America, formerly British Guiana. Like Lawrence and Lorne and our students who were tucked away in their Balinese villages decades later, most of us Peace Corps volunteers were tucked away in rural villages along the coast of Guyana. Also, like the Blair brothers and our students, we were absorbed into these villages.

We were the first Peace Corps group to go to this country, rich in cultural diversity, but suffering from centuries of colonization. Our job was to give this new nation a boost by providing math and science teachers for rural high schools and architects for various projects being initiated throughout the country.

Our two-month training at Howard University in Washington, D.C., happened quickly. None of us learned much about Guyana, but we did begin learning how to open to people from different cultures. The cardinal rule was to stay flexible.

We entered Guyana knowing that we had to be sensitive to their newly-declared independence. Our director, Ward Hower, like my dad, was a giant of a man with bushy eyebrows and black curly hair standing six-foot-three. He had a look that was quite severe but was substantially softened by his sense of humor and his affinity for storytelling.

He was adamant that he did not want to see us in his office or hanging out in the rum shops in the capital city of Georgetown but wanted us immersed in our villages. He was particularly skillful at "sniffing out" political agendas coming out of the U.S. embassy and taught us how to identify and stay clear of such activities.

From his perspective, we were in Guyana to teach high school students in the rural areas and create buildings in the capital city. As I remember, Ward's directive was: "Make good relationships. Get to know your families and the other people in your community. They will tell you everything you need to know."

His final words to us as we left for our assignments were something like this: "You will not see me…and I do not want to see you." Every six months, we volunteers gathered with the staff members, and they reminded us that "life unfolds as it does" and that the best path for the volunteer was to learn to go with the flow.

Also, we learned that there were no heroines, no heroes. We were to "work with what we had." We were to embrace the notion "that excellent teaching does not require the best textbooks or even any textbooks at all." Ward gave us the freedom to trust ourselves and our relationships.

David and I stepped into a "second world." For the previous ten years, I had lived in Mississippi where black and white people were scrupulously separated. The wall of apartheid dominated that society and was impenetrable.

I did not think about this at the time, but the Peace Corps provided me with a way to open into a larger world. In Guyana, I moved freely and interacted with anyone I wished. I was free to explore a second way of being and I was happier than I had ever been in my life.

Our director insisted that we could "make a difference" if we were willing to ride the unfamiliar. He assured us that we would be homesick and lonely, that we would be uncomfortable in the heat and in the outhouses, that the mosquitoes would be unbearable at times, and that our first day of teaching would probably be terrible.

But underneath his words I heard: "Take a chance. Fall in love. Let your world open out into the world of others. Be creative. Transform the violence."

David was assigned to Mabaruma, a remote village in the Northwest District, and I, to a village far from him that bordered a sugar plantation lying along the coast. Most of his students were Amerindian (the indigenous people of Guyana) and African (their ancestors came from West Africa as enslaved people in the nineteenth century). The people of my East Indian village were Muslims and Hindus (their ancestors came from India arriving as indentured servants at about the same time). By living and working in these rural villages, we came to know the Guyanese people, what they loved, how they struggled, what they hoped for. For most of us volunteers, our villages became our homes.

David and I fell in love. We were not going to be separated. And we did not want to return to the United States. Ward came through for us again—he asked us if we would like to stay on an additional year, train the incoming volunteers in Trinidad, and then spend the remaining year in Mabaruma. We said "yes" and married in Georgetown, Guyana, on June 15, 1968.

Like the Blair brothers and our students, we volunteers were drawn into something far removed from mainstream America. We became part of something larger than ourselves, a world different from anything we had ever known.

Besides working with the incredible people of Guyana, we also had a chance to get to know one another. We knew we were not going to change the world, but many of us bought into the idea that we *could* make a difference. We were a bright, creative, feisty bunch and I never met a group of people I loved more. When it was time to fly home, I said to David, "Promise me that we will return to Guyana."

Five decades have come and gone since then, and we have not returned. But it was our families and friends in Guyana who inspired us to explore Bali, to enter "the unknown" once again, and settle into that which was unfamiliar.

And once again, we found families—Balinese families—who welcomed us as their own and guided us gently into their world.

3
The Gift

On the southern edge of Bali at certain times of the day, Sanur beach swells with people; hawkers selling their wares, tourists adjusting their swim suits, scorching in the sun, hotel staff calmly attending their visitors. Millions of tourists come here every year. The developers took more than their share of the coastal land, but the beach belongs to the people of Bali. At sunrise on a clear morning you can see the magnificent volcanic mountain to the east, Mt. Agung, the highest mountain on the island and home of the Gods of Bali. She holds the mother temple, Besakih, in her arms which in turn provides homes for hundreds of smaller temples, each representing a Balinese family. Every family on the island will make a pilgrimage here, often several times a year.

The bay opens out into the Indian Ocean. To the east lie what looks like a mirage, the island of Lombok. Closer and still toward the east is the sacred island of Nusa Penida. The god on that island communicates directly with the gods of Bali; informing, healing, reprimanding. Stretched next to Nusa Penida, but closer to the Sanur beach is Lembongang, best known for its seaweed farms. All of this lies before us. We watch the ships go by and soak in the last bit of quiet before the hawkers take hold of the strip.

In the quiet of this bay we were resting after our flight. Our hotel was a tiny kingdom of miniature palaces and fragrant gardens.

One of these tiny palaces was ours. Its exquisitely carved front door opened to a narrow staircase leading to a spacious room illuminated by a wall of beautifully proportioned windows. I slumped onto the bed and listened to the waves and the doves.

My right hip was throbbing and I was seeking water. Before I'd left for this trip, my physician informed me that I had degenerative arthritis and would need hip replacements. Surgery was postponed until later. "You are too young," he said. Namely, if I had my hips replaced at fifty-two years of age, the prosthetics would have been worn out by the time I became an old lady.

I thought about the swimming pool I had spotted on our way in. I yanked my swimsuit from my suitcase, jumped into it, and headed for relief. As I grew closer to the pool, I realized that the sun was as intense as the pain in my hips. But as I stepped into the water, the white, fragrant blossoms of the frangipani trees dropped around me. I moved into the water and slipped onto my back.

A woman about my age approached me. "Massage?" she said with a smile. I felt shy as she indicated with her hand that I could lie on a lounge chair and she could go to work. I guess I agreed to the massage, although I never remember saying yes to "Suzie." This was not her real name, of course, but one she'd chosen to make it easier for Western tourists to address her.

I laid down on the lounge chair on my stomach and she sat down beside me. We worked together to get my swimsuit pulled down enough so she could go to work. Our connection began with her first touch on my lower back. She started by rubbing a salve into my right hip and buttocks.

She showed me a small circular tin about three inches in diameter and a couple centimeters high. Across the top was written "Silver

Clove." She held the contents a little closer to my nose so that I could take in its aroma. The clove and menthol penetrated deeply into the tissue around my hip joint and brought a welcomed fire to the spot. *Had I told her that my hip was hurting?* Probably not, as she did not know English and I did not know Bahasa Indonesian.

Her hands, drenched in coconut oil, began to glide over my body—never stopping, knowing just where to go. She knew just how much pressure to bring to every part of my body. This continuous stream of strength and warmth spread over and into my body until I rested in a deep and timeless stillness.

Finally, Suzie lifted her hands from my body and motioned for me to sit up. Then, she brushed my hair slowly, gently, as a mother might do for her little girl. This was the first time I remembered anyone ever brushing my hair. I did remember a nun, however, stabbing a hairpin into my scalp, attempting to attach a floppy lilac to thin bits of my hair and my feeling quite ashamed because my hair could not hold the lilac. Suzie, on the other hand, had a spirit quite different from that of Sister Frances Marie. With the skill of an artisan, she took my straggly bits of wet hair, wove a braid a river long, and placed it gently over my shoulder next to my face.

I have had dozens of massages over the eight decades of my life, but I have never been touched with such care. I cannot say how it happened that I experienced such nurturance. I cannot say how Suzie opened my heart. She came to earn a few rupiah for her family but I had been touched by a healer, a loving soul who appeared from nowhere.

Suzie was the perfect person to introduce me to Bali, its beauty, its gentle people, its beautiful culture, and its heart. To this day, I keep the tiny tin of "Silver Clove" tucked away in my drawer next to my lipstick.

#11 Small Street.

4
#11 Small Street

The Pertiwi Hotel has an open-air lobby. Wicker chairs with pretty poufy cushions are set about to invite visitors to stop and take a rest. The chairs are comfortable but my stomach is not, which is often the case when I am about to meet someone new. We left Sanur Beach yesterday and traveled here today to Ubud, the arts and cultural center of Bali. For centuries, people have come here to meet the healers, dancers, painters, and musicians of the island. We are here to meet someone who knows someone. We stare into the lush gardens. A warm, spongy-like softness settles around us, an atmospheric blend of heat and moisture.

David was supervising students at the University of Vermont Counseling Center when he met Laura. She learned we were going to Bali and wanted us to stay at #11 Small Street, also known by visitors as Aji Lodge.

As a high school student, she'd been accepted into a Balinese dance program sponsored by the School for International Living and had lived with Aji and Ibu and their family. "You must stay with my Balinese family," she insisted.

Aji approached us with a smile as we lingered in the gardens at Pertiwi. After introductions, he asked us to come and stay with his family. "My son-in-law is waiting in the car to bring us there," he said. "I will help you with your bags."

David was primed and ready to go. I, on the other hand, was squirming internally. *Did they have an indoor toilet? What about a mosquito net and a fan?*

Within minutes, however, we agreed to drive to the *banjar* (community) of Tebesaya, a part of the village of Peliatan. We slipped through a tiny iron gate at the front of the compound where the family was waiting for us—a grown daughter, Kris, her husband, Cok Ahlit, their two young boys, Cok Day and Cok Surya, and Aji and Ibu's son, Ngurah.

This quiet compound formed a narrow rectangle running east to west straight to the riverbank where the land plunged abruptly into the water. Aji told us that along the bank lived the demons, the lower characters of the spirit world that needed continual appeasement from those of us who shared their space.

Ibu, along with her daughter, Kris, prepared small offerings of rice placed on tiny square platters of palm leaf. These offerings were placed on a small altar by the riverbank and at other designated spots.

Neighbors lived across the river hidden in a dense forest of bamboo and monster trees. Mostly, it was quiet there except for the occasional roar of a chain-saw. We stayed in a bungalow close to the family.

I was initially terrified to be by the river. On auspicious occasions, when people were preparing for temple celebrations, we could hear the squealing of a pig about to be slaughtered. I was told dragon-like lizards flopped around in the river bed. I never saw the giant lizards, but at night when all was black, I swear I could hear them.

During the day, we heard cheerful sounds—children laughing as they splashed in the water, and women gossiping as they soaked,

David & Aji with grandsons Evan and Abbe.

The boys playing at #11 Small Street.

squeezed, and sloshed the weekly wash into oblivion.

I liked to linger in the cozier part of the compound, near the small street and the enormous rambutan tree. Aji's grandsons kept continual surveillance of this tree. When the fruit grew to the size of a small plum, its hairy-looking surface turned scarlet and was ready to eat. The boys bit into the tough skin, felt it split and pop open. The fruit's sweet white flesh was stripped from its large pit until the boys were satiated.

If you stood under this tree and looked east, you saw a small open air pavilion called a bale. Its shiny, rust-colored tile floor was four feet off the ground, its dimensions roughly ten by twelve feet. Four corner posts held the sweeping sections of a curved roof.

When a family member died, the body was placed in the bale on a platform and attended until burial or cremation. At other times, in the heat of the day, this same space was used by Aji's grandsons for daydreaming. Once I saw them making gigantic kites there. Another time I watched them create a miniature Barong, the fun loving, lion-like fellow who roams the villages on auspicious occasions, shaking blessings on everyone.

In this bale, Aji also taught his grandsons how to play the Balinese bamboo gamelan and the Balinese flute. Sometimes in the early morning or late afternoon, neighbors dropped by and sat along the edge of the bale to exchange village news.

Close by was a kitchen walled on two sides. It held knives for chopping, a mortar and pestle for pulverizing, herbs and spices for cooking, utensils for eating and drinking. Clear glass mugs with pink plastic lids had a shelf all their own.

When the neighbors visited, the mugs were brought forth filled with hot sweet ginger tea. When the stove was lit, the smell of the wood burning took me back to a time—ancient—when Aji & Ibu's ancestors might have made the same fire and cooked the same food.

North of the kitchen was the small family temple, open to the sky. Anthurium lilies formed a white, waxy necklace around the temple's stonewall. Frangipani trees grew in the northwest and northeast corners.

As you entered the temple on the left, a small bale stood where Ibu and her daughters prepared offerings daily, some of which were placed on the landing of our porch. Set about in the small temple courtyard were multiple altars, each one tall and narrow, sculpted with images to transport a person in prayer to a world containing all that has ever been known.

Beyond the temple, closer toward the river, were three bungalows built especially for visitors. David and I spent hours on the porch of ours staring into the rain forest, mesmerized as we listened to the birds and watched the butterflies.

The trees and plants brought color and fragrance to the compound at #11 Small Street. Aji continually shaped and reshaped the landscape. He moved about often in his bare feet, wearing shorts or a sarong and a sleeveless T-shirt. He could lug, lift, prune, and plant with the grace of a prince.

During the dry season, Ibu poured a nutritious mixture of rotting eggshells and water over the plants. The hybiscus plant, the bushy plant with a million tiny yellow flowers, the banana tree, and the palm tree from the island of Kalimantan, all were drenched with this concoction. The last time I saw that palm tree it was twenty feet high. Its brilliant red bark marked a place in the compound where, on a clear night, one could look up and see the stars of the southern cross.

Aji and Ibu were continually present to their charge of maintaining a balance in this magnificent landscape, a balance between *Sekala* and *Niskala*, between the world that we can see and the world that we cannot see that, from a Balinese perspective, includes all kinds of spirits, demons, gods and goddesses, ancestors. These two worlds move together as one, creating from energies that are both light and dark.

Being attuned to the balance or the lack of balance between these two worlds and their energies is at the core of Balinese living. Aji and Ibu tended the garden of their home with hands and hearts. Offerings were created and prayers flowed in, around, and through Sekala and Niskala until an energetic spiritual balance was reflected in every corner of the compound—a microcosm of the universe and a model of the inter-connectedness of all things.

5
The Real Bali

"I was honored to attend such an important ceremony. This experience forced me to throw away my thinking mind for awhile…I carried no camera, I brought no expectations… Everything happened simultaneously: mask dancers dancing, prayers…a parade of offerings…Everything was fluid." [4]

During our second week in Tebesaya, we spent most of our time with Aji and Ibu, their family, and their other guests. They had their own stories about why they were there. Fiona and Sandra, backpackers from Australia, were just beginning a six-month journey heading next to Vietnam, then to Cambodia. We never heard Carl's story, but he and Shioda spun a relationship that looked like that of a father and son, talking endlessly about politics and economics. Shioda smoked cigarettes continuously and Carl tried to convince the old man to stop. Shioda had trained Japanese fighter pilots in WWII and was stationed in occupied Bali during part of the war. He had returned and was making his home in Bali. We never talked about his time in Bali during the war, but we knew that his wife had died shortly after the war ended.

L-R: Fiona, the author, and Sandra, a photo taken before we attended the Odalan ceremony at the village temple with Aji and friends.

We enjoyed each other's company and were beginning to learn that seeing the sights was not nearly as compelling as hanging out with each other.

During that same week, *Odalan*, a festival celebrating the anniversary of the village temple, was to take place. The village leaders agreed we could all attend with Aji as our guide.

To prepare for this, we dressed in *adat*, the traditional dress of the Balinese people. So much of being in Bali is about taking things in, not grabbing for experience but just allowing oneself to feel the energy of experience as it emerged, a notion that confounds most westerners. Aji explained that by our wearing adat, we would communicate to the people of Tebesaya our respect for their culture. He was helping us understand where we were, how we were being seen, and how we could take part in his world.

I was standing before Ibu feeling a little nervous as she gathered *sarong*, *kebaya*, and *sabuk*. She was to make me and the other ladies presentable to her god and to the neighbors. First, we were asked to take a *mandi*, or bath.

The Balinese bathing area contained a large clay vat just large enough to hold a few gallons of water. A plastic scoop floated on the top of the water and soap was reachable. I began by yanking off my clothes and hanging them on a plastic hook behind the door. The floor of the mandi room was always wet this time of day and squeezing my toes into the tile was a useless strategy. Only luck would save me from slipping across the tiles and landing in a lump at the foot of the water vat.

I began scooping and splashing water until I was thoroughly drenched. I snatched the hard clump of soap and began rubbing it all over my skin until I was completely covered with a film of slimy suds and continued scooping and splashing, delighted with my success.

Mandis are deliciously refreshing. All Balinese people take a mandi twice a day—in the morning and late afternoon. Often when I walked through the village around 4:00 p.m., I heard, behind the compound walls, the scooping and splashing. If the kids were bathing, there were giggles and squeals or pleas of mercy if the water was too cold.

Fiona, Sandra, and I were clean now. Next step was to brush our hair and tie it back neatly. Ibu chose to dress me first probably because I was the greatest challenge. She had to make her daughter's sarong and kebaya work for me. Her daughter was 5'4". I am 5'10".

The sarong, a piece of cotton material, four feet by five feet, had vibrant, jet black, stylized Bali birds and lotus blossoms that popped through a peachy-pink background. This batik was framed along the edges with strips of gold and black.

She started by wrapping my body with the sarong below the waistline (knowing if she started precisely at the waistline the sarong would be too short). I held the top corner of the sarong just slightly below my belly button, and Ibu started wrapping the sarong around me. She wanted a tight fit, so she tugged, twisted, shifted, and shaped the fabric until the last section of the material ended slightly beyond front center, the vertical edge of the batik dropping in a line straight down the front. The top corner edge of the material was tucked over the rim of the snugly wrapped material at my waist.

This was my first sarong and wearing it, my entry into Ibu's world. I stood there in my sarong and bra bundled like a baby, while Ibu slipped her daughter's peachy-pink kebaya through one of my arms and then the other. The lace kebaya was essentially a fitted long-sleeved blouse with a collar that reached up my neck. Its length covered most of my hips. The sleeves landed just a few inches below my elbow, something Ibu thought was hilarious. She continued by wrapping a piece of black material, a sabuk, two feet by four feet, over my kebaya, around my midriff, and the upper half of my hips. I slipped into my clunky sandals made in the U.S.A, the only shoes in Bali that fit my feet.

Along with the feeling of safety that came with being bundled so tightly, there was also a feeling of terror, terror born of knowing that at any moment I could unravel before the villagers and the whole world. It was only when it occurred to me that I could replicate Ibu's tugs and tucks that I regained some composure. Besides, Sandra, Fiona, and I had each other's back. Together we could handle any sarong emergency. We were now part of something that a few moments before was completely alien to us.

I was spurred on now by the tenacity of this tiny Balinese woman, who in time would become my Balinese sister, and by my two new friends Sandra and Fiona. These two were tiny like Ibu and fit as a fiddle, able to carry a forty-pound backpack into eternity. They were smart and witty and could make us laugh at the drop of a hat. Fiona had black hair and blue eyes, so Ibu dressed her in a deep purple kebaya. For Sandra, whose hair was auburn, her eyes dark brown, Ibu dressed her in a forest green kebaya.

Aji took charge of the men, dressing David and Shioda in loose-fitting sarongs and long-sleeved cotton shirts. On their heads they wore an *udung*, a cloth piece wrapped around the head and tied in an exquisite knot at the center of the forehead. Their *fontanels*, open to the sky, were accessible to the blessings of God. They wore a sash about their waist. Carl refused to wear adat, saying he had his own traditional dress. His ancestors, Muslims, were from Africa. He wore white loosely fitting cotton pants, a long-sleeved white collarless shirt and a colorful blue and white embroidered cap that sat on the back of his head. Around his waist, he wore a traditional Balinese sash, a compromise to Aji's request.

Aji had mercy on us ladies as we shuffled along in our tightly wrapped sarongs, each of us looking more like a penguin than a princess. A car picked us up and drove us to the temple. In the twilight, we climbed dozens of steps to the entrance, a stone sculpture, appearing like an inverted funnel, rose sixty feet high, twenty-five feet wide at the base, exquisitely carved in limestone. An eight foot split in the middle of the structure formed a gateway to the open air temple.

Hundreds of people of all ages were coming now, dressed in adat, each reaching the threshold and stepping through the narrow passage into the temple and the vastness of the sky. The *gamelan* (Balinese orchestra) was playing, incense filled the air, the high priest prayed, his prayer bell ringing continuously. A hundred people at a time gathered before the altar brimming with offerings.

We watched quietly from the side while others prayed. The

atmosphere was imbued with a soft, sacred quality that left us speechless. We walked slowly along the perimeter of the temple through the gentle flow of activities, time passing without our knowing. Young folks flirted with one another and in the smiles of the hundreds, the movement of people and prayers evolved without a glitch. Musicians played and young women danced gracefully as if in a dream. Children watched, relaxed and happy in their dazzling adats, holding the same soft focus as their parents. Each seemed to be looking for something. Lusty young men spotted Fiona and Sandra and called out "Cantik, Cantik!" Beautiful, beautiful. Sandra muttered, "Cheeky rascals," Fiona laughed, but all the while they wore the same smiles as those of their admirers.

Aji asked us to look toward the entrance. Passing through the narrow gateway was a single line of seven young women identically dressed in light green silk sarongs and kebaya with gold sashes, their hair tied in the Balinese knot. The young women were carrying offerings on their heads that were cylindrical in shape, about two feet in diameter and three feet high. The colors and textures of the offerings reflected the splendor of the island.

A beautifully baked crisp-skinned duck held a prominent place in the display, along with rows of shiny apples, oranges, mangoes, and rambutan. Colorful confections were tucked inside this culinary sculpture, some of which were concealed in tiny pouches of woven coconut leaf. As the women floated down the stone steps, we were motionless, entranced. The night air was warm and filled with the fragrance of flowers, the sky filled with stars. I do not know how long we stood there watching.

When it was time to leave, Aji came for us. He led us from that place like a nobleman leading his family home, all the while saying goodbye to neighbors and friends. Babies slept in their mothers' arms, the toddlers perched on their fathers' laps. The younger girls watched the older girls dancing. The younger boys were mesmerized as they listened to their fathers play the gamelan. This was a time for families all basking in the joy of their good fortune to have children and elders and ancestors.

During our time in the temple, Aji answered some of our questions, but mostly he reminded us to follow the lead of the Balinese people. His core instruction was to relax into the moment and learn by watching and listening.

We climbed the stone steps once more, exiting through the same narrow passage through which we entered. We were filled with the happiness that comes when you have been saturated with beauty. We were silly with euphoria, giggling as we squeezed into the tiny jeep. Sandra was on Shioda's lap, Fiona next to them, David on the other side of Shioda. I was crammed into the front seat with the driver. Carl and Aji managed to hunker down in the back. The driver started the car, and, as we rolled away, we all began to sing silly, joyous songs. It did not matter that we were squashed inside the jeep. We were happy and quite oblivious to anything other than ourselves.

Suddenly Aji wanted our attention. Politely, he asked us to quiet down. He explained that in the Balinese way, maintaining a balance of energies was most important. One should not be too happy, too sad, too angry. *Was he asking us to modulate our happiness?*

He continued by explaining that from a Balinese perspective, it is okay to experience the fullness of one's joy, but it is important to modulate its expression so that the experience of the whole is not disturbed. This was a moment, a point in time, when we were acutely aware that things were different in Bali.

As we listened to him, I could see in the headlights an accident up ahead. We were scared now. A person lying on the street, a motorbike overturned, a car to the side of the road, someone leaning over the person in the street. The driver of the car helped the young cyclist to her feet. Thankfully, it had not been a serious accident. We were shaken nonetheless.

Was Aji right? In our commotion had we scrambled the energies of the universe and thus caused this accident? We will never know, of course, but it is the kind of thing one thinks about in Bali.

When we returned to our bungalows at Aji's, I was delighted to peel off my sweaty kebaya and sarong. I reached for the scoop in the water room and splashed away. I felt at peace, happy, knowing there is more than one way of understanding and embracing the universe.

So often, Bali expanded my perspective on the world. For example, a couple years later David had a bicycle accident. He was coming down a steep hill on a gravel road near our home in Vermont. As he headed down the hill, he skidded and went flying over the handle bars. The emergency room doctors told David, whose face was still chalk white from the trauma, that his collarbone was broken. Nothing to do now but wait for the collarbone to heal. We were about to leave for Bali and I was ready to postpone the trip, but David would not hear of it. His arm was placed in a sling, immobilized, so that the collarbone could rest in the proper position to heal. We arranged for him to be transported in the airports by wheelchair.

When we arrived in Bali, the attendants were waiting for him with a wheelchair stuffed with small pillows. David was positioned in the chair, soft pillows tucked under and around his immobilized arm. He was gently ushered through the long lines queueing up for visitor visas. Our passports were processed quickly and we headed to the baggage claim area. A small fleet of young men lugged our bags onto carts and whisked us to our driver who would take us on to Aji & Ibu's home.

When we arrived in Tebesaya, one of the neighbors, the mother of a friend of ours, was picking up on some troubling energy that lingered in and around David. One of our students wrote this about her.

"I found myself intrigued by this older woman…Everyday she sat on her porch cutting banana leaves with a sharp knife. She sat silently. I smiled and said "salamat pagi," meaning "Good morning!" She smiled and I sat beside her. I knew her husband died a few years earlier. Now she devoted her days preparing offerings and praying. She had such a grace, a presence that touched something in me, that awakened something in me. (I sat with her many times in silence.) The day I left the village she gave me a flower…that small gesture…was of such value to me. I felt honored to be in her presence … I was very sad to say goodbye. I am not sure why she was so memorable. But, if I am that old one day, I hope I can sit on my porch and observe the world with such grace."[5]

This elderly mother, in seeing that David was not feeling confident, that the world had dealt him a blow, that he was not quite himself, insisted that she make an offering and pray.

This was another time when I was acutely aware that something different than anything I had ever known was about to happen. Nyoman Sujana, her son, explained that David's spirit lingered at the spot where he fell and that his spirit needed to be retrieved and reunited with his body if he was to have a complete recovery. In other words, he must return to the place of the accident.

Since he could not physically do this because the accident had occurred in Vermont, other provisions were made. A

Nyoman Sujana and David

couple of young men from the village cordoned off a spot on the street nearby Aji's house where such a reenactment could take place. Traffic respectfully moved around the designated area.

David was dressed in adat and sat on the designated spot, receiving instructions from our friend's mother. Offerings were placed there, incense was lighted, and holy water was sprinkled all over the area, especially on David's head. All the while the *mangku* (the village priest), the elderly mother, and other selected ladies saturated the environment with prayers. Like the events in the temple, this ceremony flowed seamlessly.

David never talked about this event again. In the days that followed he walked taller. His movements were more fluid, his smile more frequent. The neighbors were happy to see that David's spirit was reunited with his mind and body once again.

6
The Heat

Every morning, David and I awoke to the crisp chirp of a little bird that sat on the hybiscus bush outside our window. We were convinced it was the same bird that landed on the same bush every morning at 6:02. The chirping continued for several minutes until this bird was joined by one dove, then another, then another until a chorus of cooing filled the air, creating a soft crescendo of sound. As the cooing started to fade, the crowing of the roosters began. *Who was the conductor of* this *symphony? How many roosters were there? One hundred? Two hundred?* The crowing gradually became less frequent, then silence. From that moment on, the sun warmed the atmosphere rapidly. People went about their chores slowly.

Noel Coward wrote a song in the 1930s that rang out, "Mad dogs and Englishman go out in the midday sun…" This satirical song pokes fun at the English and their naivete about tropical heat. Unlike the Englishman, the Balinese do not go out in the midday sun, advising "*Pelan…pelan,*" which means "Slowly…slowly."

Seduced by the beauty of the tropics and driven by a curiosity about almost everything around me, I often did not heed this warning and ended up collapsed in my bed, my entire body aching. Nauseated and befuddled with chills and fever, I sputtered something like, "Oh, I must have the flu." I learned that if I drank two quarts of water over a period of fifteen minutes, I felt somewhat normal again. This happened to me a few times before I realized that, indeed, I did *not* have the flu but something more like heat stroke. I learned quickly that *matahari* (the sun) calls the shots in this part of the world.

The tropical heat taught us to tolerate stillness, to appreciate inactivity, to observe with no object in mind. "Hanging out" is a way of life in Bali. The heat dominates as the inner world quiets down. In fact, the heat plunked me into the present moment. I learned that the mind becomes calmer as activity slows down. The mind bows to the heat, suspends analysis, and allows the external world to speak in its own way.

When it was too hot to move, I was drawn to whatever activity was taking place before my eyes. I learned mosquitoes disappear around noon just about the time the ants, the butterflies, and dragonflies arrive.

These creatures seem unaffected by the heat. At high noon one day, I watched ants working on my porch as they formed a moving line coming from two different points. When two ants met, there was a kiss, then each moved on in opposite directions. Over and over again, I watched as pairs of ants met, kissed, and continued on their way. I watched for quite some time until I understood. They were communicating. *What do ants communicate with a kiss in the noonday sun?*

Another afternoon, I kept my eyes on the bush that was continuously in bloom just beyond our bungalow. The butterflies—orange, iridescent blue, yellow, reddish-brown—came like a flying rainbow. On more than one occasion in this same area, I observed two black butterflies in a spiral flight, together ascending and descending, perfectly synchronized in a fluttering whirl of energy, their wings never touching, their movements so coordinated so as to appear as one entity. They danced in this sugar of intimacy for quite awhile, and I watched for as long as the dance continued. When they flew their separate ways, I felt lonely. But, I also felt like I had witnessed something so compelling, so familiar. *What was it I had just seen?*

Sometimes the heat induces a kind of trance that invites the mind to let go, to flow with its own curiosity and spaciousness. Questions arise that never need to be answered.

Eventually, David and I found a proper rhythm for our day. In early morning hours and late afternoon, we walked about the village. In the evening, we had dinner in an open air *warung* (small restaurant). The rest of the time we visited neighbors, read, wrote, took naps on the porch. It was also a great time to have a long lunch somewhere cool with a new friend from Bali, Germany, New Zealand, Thailand, Jakarta, Corsica. Ubud was an international setting, populated with visiting artists, dancers, architects, historians, and writers who came to study and work. A Balinese friend once said, "Carla, I don't have to travel the world. The world comes to me."

7
The Rain, the Mosquitoes, and the Hospital

A little boy whose family had just arrived from Paris the day before was the first person to wake in the place called "Hidden," another spot we liked to stay in Tebesaya. He made his way to a large stone in the little garden in front of his family's bungalow. There he sat down with his ukulele, the kind you find in the local market for a few bucks.

The sky hung heavy and dark. He began to strum, creating a sound that I felt disturbed the quiet, a sound that did not belong here. *After all, people were sleeping!*

He could not see me as I peeped from my bedroom window, and I hoped he could not hear what I was thinking. I continued to watch and listen. A light rhythmic plunking accompanied his song, a delicate chant that countered the heaviness in the air.

No one ran out to stop him. He belonged here. He played for all of us. I suspect he could feel this. He was a part of all this: the neat little garden, the tiny swimming pool, the tropical forest a little in front of him that lay hidden along the edge of the river. He was a part of the squawk of the gecko, the bark of the dog, the crowing of the roosters, the symphony of doves.

Suddenly, drops of rain began to fall. Bursts of laughter came from the bungalow next door. The little boy with his strumming and chanting had summoned the rain and now it chased him back to his mom and dad.

At the same time, the rain released the young lovers from their lusty bed. The two were dancing in the rain now, the rain beating on their skin and hair. They chased one another squealing, until finally, they jumped into the tiny pool, splashing, teasing, kissing, diving. They continued to play drenched by the rain, drunk on love. The little boy and the young lovers had become a part of a village. That often happens in Bali.

Sometimes when it rains, it lasts for quite awhile, keeping villagers stretched out on their beds, listening. The sound of the rain pounding on a thatch roof always made me sleepy but not sleepy enough to snooze. Always, during the rain at Aji and Ibu's, a narrow, rushing stream formed and passed to the right of our bungalow, gaining speed on its way down to the river. As the river became swollen, it ripped away debris on the side of the banks and sent it down to meet a larger river further away. Along the river, mammoth trees, arms wide open, were thoroughly soaked and shining, ready to meet the blazing sun when it returned.

When the rain stopped, I always felt a little sad. But, I enjoyed the soggy green trees and the short period of cool that came after. An introvert, I'd spent much of my life trying to escape the world and its people. Over the decades, working as a clinical psychologist, I developed a passion for working with people one on one.

But being with groups of people, socializing, was more than a nightmare for me. The rain was a blessing—when it came in Bali, it meant I couldn't go anywhere. I could stay home with Aji and Ibu and their family. All was quiet. If the rain continued through the night, we all fell into a deep sleep.

The Balinese people only worried about rain when a ceremony was to take place. Then, they depended on people with special powers. Before—and often during—ceremonies, these people entered into deep trances and while in those trances, they are said to keep the rain from falling.

I witnessed this once when our friend, Professor Luh Ketut Suryani, entered a trance state, preparing the environment for her son's wedding. Again, the skies were dark and heavy. The rain held up and fell just after the ceremony was completed. The reader might say, " I do not believe in these things." And Professor Suryani would reply cheerfully, "No problem. Up to you."

When the rain stopped, the mosquitoes were stimulated to rise up from their lurking positions. It took me as long to learn about mosquitoes as it did to learn about tropical heat.

Mosquitoes often breed in shallow puddles and in small flower pots and are experts at camouflage. They hide by flying into zones where the background colors match their own. They fly low, way lower than the human eye. The only place I could follow the flight of a mosquito was when I was sitting on a toilet and only if the entire bathroom was painted white.

Mosquitoes like the early morning to feed. As they rear up from hell and fly close to the damp earth where they cannot be seen, they strike naked ankles or wherever they smell blood. Sometimes they draw blood several times before a half-awake victim is aware of being eaten.

These tiny vampires are hard to kill. They are swift and sneaky. Now you see them, now you don't. They can find the smallest hole in a mosquito net. Once inside the net, they can feast all night while the victim sleeps. One morning, I looked up and saw a mosquito resting comfortably in the crown of the mosquito netting, belly swollen with blood.

Mosquitoes do not linger in open spaces. Instead they settle in small dark bedrooms, in open suitcases, open drawers, behind cabinets, in closets. Even in closed air-conditioned offices, there are mosquitoes. Any time a door is opened, they fly in.

Nicky Mclean, a backpacker we met in 1996, the second year we visited Bali, was a physicist and computer analyst who took breaks in his career to leave New Zealand and travel the planet sometimes for years at a time. When we first met him at Aji Lodge, he and his buddy, Charles, were on their way through the archipelago of Indonesia. They planned to continue on through Malaysia, onto Vietnam, Cambodia, and then onto China. After China, Charles and Nicky planned to part ways. Nicky continued on traveling through "the Stans," the Middle East, the Sudan, Cameroon, Niger, Mali, Senegal, Mauratania, Morroco, Gibraltar, then on to London.

I was envious of his freedom. I sat on the porch in the back of the compound and listened to Nicky and Charles for hours. They traveled by foot, by bus, or, by any vehicle that looked like it might not break down immediately. Nicky especially adored traveling by train.

Nicky helped me understand two important things about mosquitoes in the tropics. First of all, they will bite wherever there is bare flesh. Second, one bite by an infected mosquito can make you very sick. One should cover the body and feet, Nicky told me. He wore, for example, a long-sleeved khaki shirt, khaki pants, hiking boots with substantial socks. Sometimes he wore mosquito repellent in the early morning and at twilight.

I paid attention to Nicky. He knew what he was about. After his mosquito lecture, I went to the market to find paper thin cotton material. Next, I found a skillful seamstress. She took the yards and yards of cotton and made for me loose-fitting long pants, and long-sleeved blouses that buttoned up the front with wonderful coconut shell buttons.

Some days I wore the khaki-colored outfit, next day the orange, another day the light blue. Always my blouse and pants were matching and covered me completely.

Because each outfit was made of the same paper thin cotton, I referred to them as my "paper clothes." They were comfortable and cool even in the hottest part of the day.

Mosquitoes like dark colors where they can land, and bite, and never be seen. If they landed on my paper clothes, I could see them and kill them. Sometimes I sprayed repellent on my clothes.

My routine went like this: I arose in the morning, put on one of my paper outfits, sprayed my feet, hands, and neck with heavy-duty mosquito repellent. Then I lit mosquito coils and set them on the porch. All this took place before my morning coffee.

While mosquitoes were my enemy, I became best friends with the geckos, the smaller lizards called caceks, and also the bats. These marvelous creatures chomped mosquitoes. In the evening, the geckos and caceks would travel the walls and ceilings with their suction cup feet and pounce on the mosquitoes and other bugs that gravitated towards the lights. The bats dove across the porches in the evening and gobbled as many insects as possible with each swoop.

There was a good reason I had such an obsession for hunting down and killing mosquitoes. David and I were once spending a few nights by the ocean with a family in their compound in the little village of Candi Dasa. The little bungalows were romantic except on evenings when there was no moon, the ocean was calm, and the room fell dark and hot.

On just such an evening, we removed the mosquito net, desperate to capture any breeze, unknowingly presenting a feast for the mosquitoes. In the early morning, the rain came, cooled the air, and we slept peacefully.

A few days later, I began to ache like someone had beaten me with a baseball bat. Then fierce abdominal cramping began. Our hostess said, "Carla, we need to take you to the village doctor."

The doctor watched me stagger in, listened to my plea for a bathroom, and when I returned, he spoke gently. "You must go to Sanglah Hospital in Denpasar," which was a two-and-a-half-hour drive from the village. Our hostess drove me there and stayed to translate while the young doctor poked my lower abdomen and determined after a brief exam that I had appendicitis. He explained he would prepare me for surgery. Meanwhile, David called our friend, Yuni, also a doctor.

A couple years before this event, Yuni and her fellow resident, Yaya, the son of Prof. Suryani, our colleague, stayed with David and me in Vermont for six months. They became an integral part of our family and the family of professionals at The Counseling Center at the University of Vermont. David and Suryani had envisioned this to be a fruitful collaboration, and, of course, it was.

When Yuni arrived, she asked the young physician if he had tested for dengue fever. When he said no, she explained that gastrointestinal distress can often accompany dengue fever. Even in my delirium, I sensed Yuni was now in charge. She was a brilliant doctor with a presence, clear and sharp, an integrity that was always in the foreground, and a mind attuned to details. Quickly she saw the whole picture and managed without a fuss to get me away from the eager young surgeon. Results confirmed that I had dengue fever.

Suryani was known to the Balinese people as Professor Luh Ketut Suryani—the most esteemed title for any person on the island. She was head of the Department of Psychiatry at Udayana University, where she was teaching, doing collaborative research, writing books. She also worked in her own private practice and was a prominent leader on the island, appearing weekly on television and speaking frequently on the radio, opening discussions about the needs of the elderly, the many aspects of drug addiction, the importance of education that fostered creativity and confidence, how to nourish relationships in the family, how to strengthen the Balinese culture in the modern day world, and the negative influences of the western world. She was a stellar leader in the domain of preventive medicine and community-based health and founder of the Suryani Institute of Mental Health. She expected her residents to be committed to the health and healing of all the people on the island, a legacy of public service she inherited from her father.

In her twenties, Suryani married a prince, a member of one of the royal families of Bali and adhered to the letter to her role as wife of a prince. During the next decades, she also gave birth to six sons, graduated from medical school, studied abroad, took her place at Udayana University, and initiated her private practice.

At an open air pavilion near the Parliament Building in Denpasar, she offered free weekly sessions in meditation training. She has always been known as a political activist with no tolerance for corruption in the government. Beloved by her people and her many friends and colleagues throughout the world, she is without a doubt a giant amongst us. Her love for her people and her culture is boundless.

But, when she came into that room to see me, I saw my friend.

She stayed with me for hours each day for several days as did Yuni. Suryani was adamant that I keep drinking fluids. And, one did not say no to Suryani. She was also insistent that I eat, as dengue fever induces anorexia. The stomach revolts at the thought of swallowing anything. As she sat next to me, she held my upper arm tightly in one hand while the other scooped porridge from a bowl to my lips.

She was relentless. I felt like she was saying to me, "Carla, you are not going to die—not on my watch." I can remember begging her to stop but she did not—not until she was confident that I had had enough food to sustain me.

Any time she entered the room, she wanted data: "What was my temperature? What were the most recent blood counts?" David, Yaya, and Suryani's husband Cok Ahlit sat on the couch, while she peeled off instructions. "Bring fluids…The IV is not working…We need ten bottles of Pucari Sweat."

I don't remember much about the next days. I knew Suryani was there often. I kept feeling her firm grasp on my arm and each time I connected with my own strength. "You must drink this much," she would say as she pointed to a level on the bottle.

In my fever frenzy, I wanted her to go away. But she did not. "You must drink more." My veins were collapsing. She confronted the nurses. They had hooked up my IV improperly and fluid was not dripping into me. The blood count needed to be checked. My blood cells were being destroyed by the virus that was injected into me by mosquitoes.

It was a dangerous time. Hydration was one of the biggest challenges. No pain medication could be used. I was so sick that I really didn't know I was sick. The fever took over. David stayed with me and slept on the small couch each night. There was nothing to do but wait. Suryani popped in to check on my latest blood counts. She continued with me off and on for over a week.

On the eighth day, my blood count numbers sank to rock bottom, and then started to climb. When the numbers started to change, it was quite a dramatic event, leaving friends and the doctor to feel quite triumphant. I had survived dengue fever. The body—and Suryani—had worked relentlessly to return me to a healthy state.

A couple years passed and David and I were again relaxing in our favorite Balinese village by the sea. I looked over at David stretched out in the lounge chair and noticed he was covered with splotches that looked very much like hives.

By the time we got to the hospital, David's fever was soaring. and he, too, tested positive for dengue fever. The symptoms started with hives, which Suryani assured us was quite common.

This time we knew the drill. Suryani made sure everything was set up for his care, and she headed for home. I slept in the little bed by the wall a short distance from David. While I was stretched out on the bed, I spotted and swatted mosquitoes. The bastards flew low next to the wall where a small purple light plugged into the outlet near the floor gave off a stinky perfume that I think was supposed to attract and possibly kill the mosquitoes.

I hunkered down by the tiny light and smashed as many mosquitoes as I could. I continually monitored the IV as I was instructed. Suryani tried to persuade me to come home with her, reassuring me that David would just be sleeping for the next days. She monitored his condition each day, but I told her I would stay in the hospital for the duration.

The next day, our village learned that David was in the hospital and an entourage led by Aji arrived in David's room. David gave them a feeble wave and passed out. Each one of the group found a spot either on the couch or on the floor, establishing themselves in the hospital room as if they were visiting a brother. Some brought snacks and water. As they talked, I thought, *How can David rest with all this socializing going on?*

Aji walked around the corridor leading all newcomers into the room. More arrived and took their place on the floor, each smiling and greeting one another as if they were at a party. I could not believe it. Their voices were at a low roar now while David slept motionless.

In our Western culture, when someone is sick, maybe one or two might stay with the sick person. In Bali, dozens show up until either death or recovery comes. Balinese people do not like to leave their family members alone.

As a Westerner, I wanted my husband to have rest. I felt like I was in a strange land. People were not being quiet. And, it was clear they had no plans to leave. I was becoming more and more tense. Finally, I spoke with Aji in the corridor. I did not want to offend him, but I also wanted David to have quiet. I asked Aji if he could ask the folks to leave for the day.

When I walked back into the room and looked at the people there, I realized I was looking into the faces of our dear friends. In my fear and anxiety, I had forgotten this. These were the people who worked tirelessly with us, helping David and me provide the most amazing experiences for our students. These were the people who cared for the students and welcomed each one with complete acceptance and love.

When Aji returned to the group, he said, "David will sleep now." Graciously, one by one, our friends asked David for permission to leave. "Ti ti yang mah parmit." David nodded to each.

That is the way it is in Bali. When you leave, you don't just blast your way out of a gathering. You ask permission to leave.

8
Sang Yang Dedari
The Dance of the Little Angels

In the mountains near the village of Kintamani, the air was cool and the fog was rolling in. I was perched on the ledge of a bale situated in the village temple, dressed in adat, waiting. Next to me was a tall British guy, who was as curious as we were about what was to happen. Peter, also a friend of Suryani, had white hair although he was only in his mid-forties.

He turned to me. "What is the medal that you are wearing?" he asked.

"My mom was a Benedictine oblate," I explained. "She wore this as a symbol of her devotion to the teachings of St. Benedict. She died last year, and I claimed it for my own."

We talked for awhile discovering that we both had been brought up in the Roman Catholic Church, enjoying its rituals, particularly the Mass, the recitation of Latin prayers, and the sound of Gregorian chant. This was a gentle moment, one in which it felt like a friendship was forming. Suryani had invited all three of us, as well as a young photographer, Carl, to attend the event. She was working on a book about Balinese ceremonies and trance.

David and Peter and I had no idea what was coming.

We were still sitting on the edge of the bale when the villagers, also all dressed in adat, began moving, gathering, so as to form a wide circle around the key players. Older women were attending two young girls dressed in sarongs, sabuk, kebaya, all white, giving them the appearance of little angels. A chorus of women and two young men gathered near the priest.

The three of us were part of the circle now, viewing the open space. We could see the little girls kneeling in front of the priest, focused on a tiny, spinning doll. The handmade dolly, constructed with layers of soft cotton, had two narrow cords tied to its waist, each a couple feet long and each one pulled to each side of the doll.

Somehow, the strings were tied so that when the two attendants of the priest pulled these cords, the doll began to spin. The two young girls held their focus there, while the thick smoke of incense curled around their young bodies and the older women attended to the details of the offerings.

The priest prayed, and the two girls—eyes closed now—began slipping into a trance, seemingly going deeper and deeper with each ring of the prayer bell. The gamelan was playing, and the chorus of women were chanting.

In the next moment, simultaneously, the girls arose from their kneeling position and began to dance—their movements fluid, natural, exquisitely beautiful, and synchronized. At this same time, I saw on the edge of the crowd on the other side of the circle, a woman standing behind a tiny girl. When the two little angels danced, the woman reached down and held the arms of the toddler in the same position as that of the two dancers. As the two young dancers changed their position, the woman moved the little toddler's arms to match the new position of the dancers. It occurred to me that I was watching the transmission of this ceremony from one generation to the next, a ceremony that had been passed on just this way for a thousand years.

As the ceremony continued, it felt as if we were all being pulled into the energy of the dancing girls. The people watched for *taksu*, the moment in which the spirit of the goddess entered the young girls. After a while, the two were gently lifted, positioned so that they could easily climb onto the shoulders of young men. Deep in trance now, the girls stood perfectly straight, eyes closed, faces relaxed, expressionless.

David, Peter, and I were motionless. The community formed a tighter circle around the girls, everyone slightly touching one another. The gamelan continued playing as the thick smoke of the incense continued to envelop the girls.

Then, something unbelievable happened. The girls began to bend backwards effortlessly, again in perfect synchronicity, as if their spines were made of rubber. We watched them bend back like this until we observed sharp curves in their backs.

I thought they would surely fall. They did not. And then, just as remarkably, the girls gradually straightened up again, their eyes still closed, still deep in trance.

From the Balinese perspective, the goddess had taken possession of the girls and, in the process, was bestowing many blessings upon the village. At some point, the girls were removed from the shoulders of the young men. The people from the circle moved closer, except for the three of us. Then the little girls fell back into the arms of the older women, the priest prayed, the bell rang, holy water was sprinkled until gradually and gently the girls came out of their trances. The priest, the chorus of women, the women attending the girls, the dancing girls, the young men upon whose shoulders the girls stood, and the entire community had done their part to honor the goddess who brought blessings to their village.

Once the girls resumed normal consciousness, Suryani asked them if they remembered what they had done while in trance. Both said no. In fact, they were surprised to discover from members of the community that they had danced so beautifully, so effortlessly, so spontaneously—neither of them had ever studied dance. One of the girls did remember hearing the singing of the women. Later, Suryani told us that their training for this event only entailed prayer routines and the practices of good behavior and good speech.

When the ceremony ended, I felt at peace for the first time in quite a while. I also felt a strong connection with this community and with David and Peter. We felt so privileged to be a part of this auspicious occasion and to be given the opportunity to listen with our whole being.

David and I were beginning to understand how the Balinese live in two worlds simultaneously—the world of the seen and the world of the unseen. To stay with the energy of this community, to follow as the Balinese follow with an open heart, meant we had to let go of the need to understand everything. We needed simply to be.

9

The Dancing Circle

"The world in which you were born is just one model of reality. Other cultures are not failed attempts at being you; they are unique manifestations of the human spirit."[6]

David and I placed the comfy couches and chairs in a circle. We were preparing for the first of three classes that would take place on the campus of the University of Vermont before we headed to Bali with our students.

We usually met at the Multicultural Center which provided all manner of support for international students. In the evening, the place was quiet with only a student or two studying in a far corner or someone washing dishes in the communal kitchen. During class these students stayed on the periphery of our activities but joined us at break. I always brought cookies baked fresh that afternoon, filled with dark chocolate chips, macadamia nuts, and dried Michigan cherries. The students stood around the big, old, wooden table near the entrance to the kitchen and ate until they were satiated. David poured the apple cider and wondered how these folks would fare with avocado lassies and *nasi goreng*, the comfort foods of Bali.

Because it was not possible for David and me to spell out the real challenges of this journey in a course description, we met with each student individually before this class.

"This trip is not for everyone. It is not a vacation. In fact you will see no beaches on this trip unless we are going to a ceremony on the beach," we told them.

"You leave behind all that is familiar. When you experience culture shock as the new experiences come at you with the speed of light, you lean into the group for support, and the others in the group lean into you. You use all of your resources to step up and keep your focus on connecting with your Balinese family and your adopted village.

"You will be outside your 'comfort zone' much of the time. How do you handle intense heat? Do you have medical conditions that we need to know about? How do you feel about being with people whose language is different from your own? Can you coexist with insects? How do you feel about having very little contact with family and friends while you are gone?"

In these heart-to-heart talks, we were looking for those who might flinch and for those who might be potential whiners. We found none. Instead we became aware of how hard these students had been working to become mental health counselors, nurses, physical therapists, teachers, nurse practitioners, and they were tough. They were not afraid of hard work, and they carried a deep commitment to learn more about health and healing and cultural diversity. They genuinely wanted to learn about another world, its people, its culture, and its environment. They knew that they would have to take some risks to learn how to meet differences. They were looking for adventure and fresh ways to approach the world and their lives.

Many of them were aware that there was much more to learn, and they wanted to go to Bali to learn it. Now they were fired up, motivated, and with a nod from us, grabbed their backpacks and were out the door to sign up for the course. Around 7:00 p.m., the students wandered in and took their spots in the circle. Their faces were drawn, reflecting an exhaustion they carried like a torch. The semester had worn them down and now they were hacking away at their end of term papers and cramming for final exams.

The plan now, however, was to travel to the other side of the planet, to explore this second world. We needed to agree on how to do this, how to move in this new terrain, and how to move with each other. Officially, this was a UVM course designed to heighten intercultural awareness and to develop intercultural communication skills. The Balinese people and the members of our group formed the learning community. It was time now for David and me to prepare the students for this circle and the place we returned again and again.

When I was tottering on the edge of changing careers in the mid 1970's, I attended a conference at a small hotel in Shelburne, Vermont. The topic was "Parenting and Communication in the Family," a real snorer for most folks. Virginia Satir, however, the key note speaker and the woman who later was proclaimed "The Mother of Family Therapy" kept us on the edge of our seats.

This woman really understood human beings, and she wanted us to understand as well. Her lecture turned magical rather quickly as she used humor and theatrics to pull us into the world of human communication and the dance of speaking and listening.

"Listen as if you are looking at a painting, a painting that is emerging from the mind of the person talking to you," she said. "You try to replicate this painting, this picture, in your own mind. Make sure you take in the entire canvas. If there is any part of the painting that you cannot see clearly, ask, 'What is this? Can you tell me more about this part? I don't quite see this piece.'

"The person speaking creates their reality before you. You, the listener, the lover of truth, just takes it all in. You stay curious as the painting comes into focus, unique and ever changing, standing on its own vitality, and needing no analysis, interpretation, or judgment."

I was hooked. *Could I listen to people this way? Could I help others listen this way?*

Now, a couple decades later, we were asking our students to experiment with these same ideas. We had the students stand up, move around, pick a partner, pluck a chair from those stacked in the corner, find a spot, and sit directly across from one another—a nerve racking process for students. The mind goes wild. *Who shall I pick? Will someone pick me? How long is this thing going to last?*

Then David and I invited the students to listen the way that Virginia suggested so many years before. We posed the question: "What is it that drew you to this course?"

The dancing partners began, one speaking/painting, one listening. The atmosphere was filled with stories, coming slowly at first. In this stream of thoughts and feelings one could hear phrases like:

- "It is exciting for me to do something so spontaneous and out of the ordinary."
- "I am nervous about how it is going to be for me to be in situations in which I do not know what is going on."
- "I do hope I don't get sick. But I want to see if I can do this, if I can manage. I want to test myself."
- "I am looking forward to learning how to meditate and how to be part of a group."
- "I want to do something that will wake me up to the beauty of the world around me. School has been such a grind lately, and I feel like I have lost sight of what I am really about."
- "I have never been out of the country and I feel a bit nervous, but excited, too."

The stories continued for fifteen minutes. Then I asked the dancers to stop and switch roles. The speakers/painters now became the listeners, the listeners became painters. David and I continued to watch. The new listeners focused and let their curiosity drive their questions, while the painters came alive.

- "I have never taken a class like this before…I have always played it safe…from day one of college I've known what classes I would take… my next step always planned. This is how I felt comfortable. This will be different."
- "I was thinking I wanted to have an overseas experience and was thinking a semester. But, when I read that we would be staying with Balinese families, this seemed more like the adventure I was looking for."
- "I am coming out of a rocky relationship and, honestly, I am looking forward to getting away from school work and my relationship and stepping away from things. I think this might help me get some perspective of my life."
- "I am looking forward to learning about the members in the group and building trust with them."
- "Honestly I want to do some soul searching on this trip."

Finally, one student shared a question with which she had been grappling: "What can I do to better myself and the world around me?" Another student in her final paper wrote:

> "I was overwhelmed with everyone's presence. I was surprised that people wanted to hear about me. This experience was unfamiliar to me. The whole time I was growing up, I was a caretaker, I did for others. When people asked how I was doing, I did not know how to respond. The group was asking about me and wanting nothing in return."[7]

We could see the exhaustion draining from their faces. Smiles appeared more frequently now, and there was laughter. Juices were flowing. The sound of sharing that started like a babbling brook was now a resounding roar of storytelling. Everyone was awake. The room was filled with energy, the energy that is born when human beings are truly listening to themselves and to one another.

We returned to our circle to talk about what kind of experiences they had in the dance. "What was it like to be listened to? What was it like to speak about your own experience?"

Many talked about how hard it was at times, as the listener, to refrain from jumping in with their own story, and how hard it was at times, as the painter, to find the right words to express a feeling, a thought, or embrace a question. Some shared that they felt safe to speak freely without worrying about being interrupted or judged. Others reported that they felt relaxed now and part of the group. Some said, "As I was listening to her story I became clearer about something that was happening in me."

The students were beginning to get the feel for listening,

> "It was so natural for my mind to want to put things in categories and make judgments of others. I didn't realize how frequently I was doing this…I stopped and started listening in a new way. I'm proud of myself for learning to do this. This listening skill… allowed me to keep an open mind, to accept and value every moment … It felt so nice to be laid back and not be all twisted up in my mind."[8]

Now we needed to know that the students truly had each other's back. "Do we have a commitment from you that you will practice this dance every time you enter this circle?" we asked. "This is how we sustain our group, how we feed ourselves and each other. This is how we learn to trust one another. We are traveling to Bali not just as individuals but also as a dynamic group that will change daily as our Balinese brothers and sisters join us, and as we learn and grow and dance."

"Ibu" preparing for the opening ceremony.

10

Entering the Family Compounds
The Opening Ceremony

"It was five a.m....the streets were fairly empty... dimly lit...[we were] highly alert...Carla and David led the way...we followed close behind until they brought us to our respective families. We attempted to settle in...I just had to find my bed. It had been an exhausting journey...I was giddy with excitement about what lay ahead." [9]

"I remember immediately feeling so welcomed by the people of Bali, from the driver who took us to Tebesaya to 'Mama' who immediately took us into her home and related to us as family." [10]

"When we opened the gate, we were greeted by members of a beautiful Balinese family, Ibu Putu, Pak Ahlit, and a smiling, chubby-cheeked baby. The mother and father of the family...were incredibly welcoming...I had never experienced such hospitality and warmth from complete strangers...they treated me as if I were their family...and, this family was unlike any I had ever experienced in the western world, or even in my own family." [11]

"The first few days (in Tebesaya) provided a glimpse into the magic of Bali; Authentic Balinese cuisine at Mama's, bartering in the Ubud market, navigating the Beast (the main road in Ubud), dressing in adat, prayer in temple, tasting blessed offerings, exploring the palace, meeting a prince, watching legong dance, playing the gamelan. I eased my way into this dynamic, welcoming culture. Surrounded by smiling faces, my anxiety faded and I reached across the cultural barrier to touch the world surrounding me. I stopped fearing cultural blunders or negativity. I blended with the landscape, opening to the vibrancy around me. And as quickly as I opened, I felt received."[12]

"All of my senses were heightened, flowers and colors appeared brighter and more beautiful, the smells more aromatic, pungent. The sun felt warmer on my skin, and I felt energy coursing through my body filtering in and out from the universe. It was almost as though I was more alive than I had ever been before."[13]

The twelve students were divided among four Balinese families. After some sleep, their first assignment was to find their way to Aji and Ibu's compound at #11 Small Street. "Aji Lodge" would be where our first class meeting was held—a sign would be above the entrance.

Aji created a small room near the kitchen that became our classroom at this time of year. Large cushions, each covered with a cotton gingham of black, white, and red and representing the gods Wisnu, Shiva, and Brahma, lay in a circle around the long, low table. A sad fan in the ceiling twirled occasionally, sending a tiny breeze over the sweaty faces of the circle dwellers.

Ibu busied herself in the adjoining kitchen pouring hot tea into glass mugs with tiny pink plastic lids. She bought fresh coconut cakes from the market which she stacked neatly on a plate and placed on the table. As the students started trickling in, each found their spot and sat down on their cushion on the floor in front of the table. This would be the way we gathered for the next two weeks.

After everyone arrived, we began our time together by listening to the sounds around us: the cooing of the mourning doves, the light clattering of dishes in the kitchen, little Evan sobbing quietly because his older brother, Abbie, had gone off to school. Surrounding us were three walls covered with panels of woven palm leaves providing an exquisite background for Aji's many paintings. Each told a story about Bali's culture and its people, and about Aji and Ibu's life together. The fourth side of the room was open to the outside.

As we sat in our circle on the floor on top of the equator, Ibu placed the tray of mugs with hot ginger tea on the low table. She handed one mug to the student on her right and motioned for her to pass the mug along. Ibu repeated this action over and over at least a dozen times, until every person in the circle had a tea mug in front of them. Aji explained that in Bali, the host—in this case, him—signals the guests that they may begin drinking by removing the lid from his own tea mug. On other days, either David or I was designated to initiate the sipping of the tea. This gesture signaled that we were together now, ready to begin.

After David and I welcomed everyone, we moved around the circle, each person introducing themselves to Aji and Ibu. When everyone had spoken, David and I continued by saying how privileged we felt to be here in Bali with Aji and Ibu and with our students. Then we highlighted what we as a group had established as our way of being with each other. We reminded our students that back in Vermont we all agreed to place great attention to such things as listening with respect, staying away from analyzing one another, articulating our individual needs, speaking from our own experience and allowing others to do so, and refraining from sharing anything of a confidential nature outside of the class. We also all agreed to show up for all the meetings. Aji and Ibu listened. They were curious, relaxed, and present.

Next it was Aji's time to speak. "I was once the Commissioner of Arts and Culture in Gianyar Regency," he said, "but now that I am retired, I am the servant of Ibu," he said, laughing. He liked to introduce himself this way and tell the students of how he fell in love with Ibu, and how they came to marry one another, have two daughters, one son, and seven grandsons.

One student remembered:

"When Aji began to tell us about Ibu, I got chills. He pointed to one of his paintings which depicted the woman that was sitting by his side. 'Ibu is most important to me... If ibu gets sick for one day, the whole family stops. If I am sick for a week, no problem.' He chuckled. Aji and Ibu are soul mates, something I really did not believe in before this journey."[14]

Aji went on to say that later on that day he would take us all into his family temple, just feet away from where we were, and there we would have our opening ceremony.

Nyoman Sujana and his wife, Ibu Wati on their way home from temple.

After our meeting, Nyoman Sujana, our Balinese brother and one of the team of our field faculty, accompanied the students to a tiny shop owned by his wife, Ibu Wati. While a few girls at a time entered the shop (the guys would go later with Nyoman to select their sarong, sash, and udung), they began to glow as they gazed upon the rows and rows of sarongs.

This display was made possible by the construction and positioning of several wooden slats that looked much like curtain rods and that protruded a few inches from the wall. The first slat was positioned slightly below the middle of the wall and stretched the wall's entire width. The other slats were placed above the lower middle slat, parallel to it, and separated from each other by a few feet. The sarongs were folded many times to form a narrow swath of material that revealed both the width of the sarong and the dominant design of the batik. Folded like this, the sarongs were easily hung close together on the many rods transforming the wall of the shop into a magnificent, shimmering quilt of sarongs.

With the help of Ibu Wati, Nyoman Sujana's wife Komang, Ibu Wati's daughter-in-law, and her husband's sister-in-law, whom we all came to know as "Mama," the students selected their first sarong and sash. In the West, women often select pieces of clothing with colors that match or blend. The women in Bali often select contrasting colors, perhaps reflecting the emphasis on polarities in their cosmology. I have grown to prefer the popping contrasting colors myself, which seem to present the person as more vibrant, warm, and energetic.

There was abundant yakking and squealing going on during the students' selections. Two different languages were flying around the little shop, Bahasa Indonesian and English, but there was very little confusion. The three Balinese women encouraged, approved, and invited the students to make their selections based on how they felt when they saw and touched the fabric and the colors.

> "It felt refreshing to be encouraged by my Balinese sisters
> to take action based on what I was feeling inside."[15]

All the energy of this process gravitated towards the selection of beautiful things. What could be more joyful? The three women helped dress each student and when the girls left the shop wearing their sarongs and sashes, they stopped at Mama's warung (small restaurant) for an avocado lassie. As the lassies were slurped and the stories about their sarongs exchanged, there was an atmosphere of celebration, connection, and warmth. It would not be long now before we would all gather for the opening ceremony.

Dressed in adat, we all sat on the ledge just outside our little classroom, across from the entrance to the family temple, waiting for the *mangku* (the village priest) to arrive. We told our students that now was the time to learn as the Balinese learn. They could drop their questions and just allow themselves to feel this experience, noticing the sensations in their bodies and the energy in the atmosphere.

Tebesaya. Mangku blessing us all at the opening ceremony.

"Before the opening ceremony we all sat in front of Aji's temple and Nyoman Sujana led us through the steps of prayer and how we would incorporate flowers, holy water, and incense...In that moment I felt all my reservations melt away. We were all making a spiritual offering together to the Divine... even though I had not spiritually participated in this way before... it felt familiar..."[16]

"Om Suwastiastu Om," said the priest. "Om Suwastiastu Om," we replied. The students were a little tense and struggled a bit with the words that were so unfamiliar.

"I realized that being uncomfortable and fumbling...is a part of the experience of being in another culture."[17]

As the priest entered the temple, we stayed just outside the entrance. This is how it is done. The priest prepares the way. First he asked for permission from the gods to pray for all of us in Aji's temple. Once this permission was granted, he directed his prayers to the goddess of learning, Saraswati. For several minutes, his prayers poured forth, sounding much like a chant that comforted us and set our minds at ease.

I was told by Aji that the priest asked that the students be helped as they began their time in the village. He prayed that each student would listen well and that each would learn from their brothers and sisters in Bali. After the prayers of the priest were completed, the students were asked to enter the tiny temple and take their place on the palm leaf mats placed on the ground for this special occasion.

"As we continued the practice of collective prayer throughout our time in Bali, I could feel the prayer fill my soul each and every time."[18]

As Aji and Ibu helped the students assume the prayer posture, five inch square baskets, a few centimeters high and woven of palm leaf and filled with flowers of every color of the rainbow, were placed in front of each pair of students. Incense sticks were lit and poked in the ground next to the tiny basket of flowers.

As the incense curled upward, Aji and Ibu took prayer positions. By watching their movements, then replicating them while staying with what we were feeling, staying curious, staying open, staying with the not knowing, we learned how to participate in the ceremony.

While the prayer bell was ringing, each student placed her hands over the incense, and then folded her hands in prayer position, lifting them above her head just slightly above the third eye, a spot that marks the center of the forehead. The prayer included honoring all creatures on the earth, one's own body, all people, and all spirits, and one's own spirit.

When the bell stopped ringing, the hands were brought back down. This process was repeated three more times. Each time, a different configuration of the rainbow flowers were held between the middle fingers, the hands again raised to that place just above the third eye, and another prayer was said. All the while, students were to keep their eyes on Aji and Ibu.

When the prayers were finished, the mangku blessed each student by sprinkling holy water three times over each of their heads. Then, each student placed his right hand over his left hand, forming a cup. The holy water was then poured into this cup and sipped. This process was repeated.

The third time the holy water was poured, the water-filled hand was raised to the top of the head and allowed to soak the hair and splash down the front and sides of the face. Three more flicks of holy water over each head sealed the blessing, clearing the path for the next blessing to take place.

The rice blessing was performed by Ibu, who stood before each student and placed rice on the third eye and the throat. She also placed one grain of rice in each hand and asked that it be swallowed. She placed flowers behind each ear and threaded them through the tight strands of hair on each head. David and I observed our students, their faces soused in holy water and covered in blossoms. Three students wrote about this in this way.

> "While I am not an overtly religious person, being surrounded by people all participating in a traditional Balinese ceremony made me feel as if someone or something was guiding me and looking over me."[19]

> "It was so easy to spend time with (the Balinese people) and feel like they had let you into their lives."[20]

There was magic in the air. The world had slowed down. The offering had been received by the gods and now it could be shared among us. There were goodies to sample—many kinds of bananas; luscious rambutan; sweet cakes, light green and pink, made with rice and palm sugar. There were crunchy delights as well, made with rice and peanuts, snake fruit, and tiny green cake rolls filled with palm sugar syrup and coconut.

Delicious. We took our time munching. There was nowhere to go, no place we had to be. We had participated in an ancient ritual.

The reasons for why the bell rang for just so long; why certain prayers were said, and why specific flowers were used at specific times had long since been forgotten. Millions of people over a thousand years had repeated this same ritual, to give thanks to their gods for the many blessings bestowed, and to provide a continuity of care and clarity of mind for those who lived on this island. The ritual undeniably tied the Balinese people to their ancestors and profoundly connected them to life itself.

Weeks before the trip, David and I had asked our students to allow the Balinese people to show us how to participate in their ceremonies. One student said this:

> "The Balinese welcomed us as guests into their family temples, and they included us in each ceremony. I have never been more touched by a complete stranger, and each experience helped me to connect with my new Balinese friends in ways I could not have anticipated."[21]

Another student noted:

> "The challenge for me was to come out of the mind and into the moment, where I could embrace the place of not knowing … once I was able to do this, I found myself more open to living in the moment and feeling the energy there with all of my senses."[22]

The students met that challenge that day. They gave up trying to understand with their heads. Instead they learned by gently being with Aji, Ibu, and Nyoman. They learned from listening to the ringing bell, smelling the flowers and tasting the delicious food, feeling the sweat on their faces and the pain in their knees. They learned, too, from the feelings of intimacy and beauty that emerged from the hearts of the folks with whom they prayed…and from the atmosphere that held them delicately in love.

Aji , teaching a student how to play the tinklet.

A student playing the Balinese gamelan with help from Balinese students.

One of our students chatting with young students

Nyoman Sujana's students guiding David and a friend through their school

Our students learning legong dance.

Our student presenting an award for outstanding scholarship, an annual
event sponsored by a educational foundation started by University of
Vermont students in 1999 and administrated by Aji.

Aji introducing the students to Balinese art and history
at the Agung Rai Museum

11
Where the Lotus Blooms

"The Nirarta Center was the most beautiful sight I have ever seen in my life. From the exotic flourishing nature all around us to the intricate yet simple bunglows, I felt as though I was in heaven. There was even something different in the air that just made me feel instantly at peace." [23]

Nirarta lies on many acres of land surrounded by rice fields that hang along the valley of the Unda River overlooked by Mt. Agung. In 2017, this volcanic mountain erupted covering the area with volcanic ash, shaking dwellings to their limit, and turning the river water into something that looked much like flowing wet cement. Decades before, in 1963, a more devastating eruption occurred there, killing hundreds when the lava flowed down into villages and into the sea.

Fortunately in the more recent eruption, the area was spared such devastation, and when the volcanic action settled down, the people returned to their normal activities. The gardener at Nirarta returned to his gardens, the farmers returned to plowing and planting. Peter, our friend and creator of Nirarta, returned to teaching and writing. Peter's wife, Putri Dayu, returned to attending to everything that nourishes this sacred land. Maya and Mira, their children, returned to university.

During the past two and a half decades, and even now, people come to Nirarta to rest, to learn, to climb the mountain to the tiny temple to find what they must find.

A student recalls:

> I retreated to the hills in front of my bungalow. And sitting on a stone step above the river, I watched the sun slowly descend feeling the most desperate and lost...*Why am I here? What am I doing?* I felt hopeless and without answers...My mind couldn't think. My mind wouldn't place me. The GPS couldn't locate my signal. I had no idea where I was going, and I couldn't quite articulate where I had been. It was in this moment that I found myself. I found everything I had been searching for. I found peace. I found God...what happened that night at Nirarta, an experience that re-centered my energy...I realized the healing was always inside of me not contained in another person, book, or sermon. God, unidentified with any sect, has always been with me, walking along side. Years of searching ended. I found my answers by simply *being.*"[24]

In earlier days at Nirarta on this same land, I remember seeing two little girls sitting with their grandmother along the side of the lotus pond, not too far from where the visitors stayed and not so far from the meditation center.

Putri Dayu and Peter's children, Maya and Mira, years ago near the lotus pond.

Little Mira and Maya hovered over the water with a piece of string, a hook tied to the end. The bait was supposed to tempt one of the tiny fish that circled the forest of lotus stems and fed upon the riches of the muddy bottom of the pond. Their grandma gently coached them not to get too close to the edge—not so much because the pond was dangerous, but because they wore their pretty flowered dresses given to them by their other grandmother who lived in Norwich, England.

The pond was filled with lotus blooms, their bright pink petals stretching open to bask in the sun. In the middle of each bloom was a magnificent, soft yellow core that caught the gaze of everyone. When the sun began to set, the petals closed, and the blooms disappeared as if they were never there. As twilight slipped into darkness, the pond began to pulsate with the melody of a hundred frogs. They were center stage now and, in this watery theatre, they croaked an opera, over-powering and vibrant, irritating some, enticing others to sleep. Those who were irritated wanted the noise to stop. "One cannot even hear oneself think," they complained.

Exactly. The frogs took us to a place where we could not think. "Nothing else, nothing else, nothing else," they croaked. "Come, be here in this beautiful place where time stands still, and the heart wants to play with the butterflies."

We were all settled in at Nirarta now. At sunrise of the next day, while the students were still sleeping, David sat in silence on the veranda of our bungalow, drinking his coffee. I made my way up the road to the top of the hill where the entire valley lay before me.

I saw a farmer in a nearby field, his hands upon the long handles of his plow hitched to a cow with a white ring around his bottom. With an awkward twist of his head, the cow looked over his shoulder, rolled his eyes back to catch a glimpse of his master behind him. The flies were biting the cow now and he was agitated. When the farmer uttered a sound, a sound I never heard before, the cow was startled, and the two lunged forward with a movement that launched the plow and left the earth unfolding into a long shiny snake.

Grampa Mike came into my mind's eye, and I thought of how much he would have loved this sight. In the spring of 1961, when I just turned seventeen, Grampa Mike came to visit my family. I had just gotten my driver's license, and he wanted me to drive him to the neighboring fields, the magnificent crops of the Mississippi Delta. As we looked out over the vast flatland, he explained to me how skillfully the farmers had plowed the land and how they had set out the planting in such a beautiful and efficient way. If Grampa had seen the cow with the white ring around his bottom, smelled the richness of the earth, and absorbed the quiet of that early morning, I suspect he might have lit his pipe and puffed the smoke into a dream of his own fields and cows he once tended in the flatlands of Saginaw, Michigan.

Mike and his wife, Mame, lived on their farm in the early part of their marriage, Mame giving birth to five daughters and one son. One daughter died shortly after she was born. They nurtured their children, their land, and their animals with an intelligence, a love, and a respect that I often see reflected in my brother's eyes and in the eyes of my cousins.

Their daughter, Mary—my mom—shared this passion for the earth. She was not so interested in planting. Instead, she enjoyed long walks in the woods and splashing in the waters of a nearby pond. Even as a child she was a dreamer and had little interest in controlling or organizing her surroundings.

Mostly she liked to feel the world, read its lessons with her senses and her heart. I think she was a bit like her grandmother, Gramma Mame, who was a psychic. This was a well-kept secret in the family—it wasn't until I was in my early forties that my mom and my aunt, Catherine, confided in me that Gramma Mame in fact had such powers. She had been portrayed to me as a gentle, enormously strong woman who could see auras and understand things that transcended time and place.

Since the Catholic priests in the area preached against such "shenanigans," the people of the town, who also knew about Gramma Mame's gifts, were complicit in keeping the secret, but came to her to relieve both physical and spiritual suffering. They came to her to receive encouragement and to listen to her wisdom. They came to her to understand more about this vast universe.

My mother had similar gifts but she used them in different ways. She was trained at Michigan Normal College in the 1930s in the methods of Maria Montessori, which emphasized kinesthetic learning and allowed children to explore the world from their own interests and inclinations.

When Dad brought our family to Mississippi in the mid 1950s, Mom decided to start her own private school, "Mrs. Newman's Kindergarten." Sometimes she and Dad took trips to the Mississippi River to gather supplies for the school. These were joyful trips, taking them away from the routines of their daily lives. The river gave them solace and something else.

They traveled to it from Cleveland, our hometown, and passed through Rosedale, making their way to the levee. When the river was not too high, there were places along the line of the levee where one could drive up and over the levee and head for the river's edge.

There, Mom and Dad found areas along the river where the earth had been ripped away by the fierce currents leaving only a small canyon of clay. Mom dug up chunks of the soft clay and placed them in two buckets. Dad poured river water over the top of the clay and hauled the buckets to the car.

The next day, Mom placed the wet clay on a long low tables in her school. The kindergarten children went to work squeezing and patting the clay, enjoying its oily surface and its wet softness. There was something compelling in that clay, something that invited the children to sculpt.

This is what Mom was about. She continually wanted to bring the natural world to her young students.

Being at Nirarta brought back these memories of my mom. Like her, I, too, loved to be in the natural environment. And, at moments in this beautiful spot atop the hill, I wanted to stay a little longer, and soak in just a little bit more of the beauty around me. I could hear the sound of the water in the irrigation canals as it roared down through the countryside, following the slope of the land and flooding the rice paddies wherever beckoned. I could see to the west a patch of blue, the South China Sea, to the east Mt. Agung.

I headed east on the road. My destination, a tiny shop. The shopkeeper, never surprised to see me, reached for a pack of *kretek*, clove cigarettes, that were neatly stacked with a million other items in a glass cabinet that sat upon the counter in his shop. Sometimes, if the moment called us to do so, we had a smoke together as we stared out into the morning light. That was a quiet moment, and private, like my moments with my Grampa Mike as we stood along the cotton rows.

Many who stayed at Nirarta found themselves taking a walk such as my own, staying on this same road and returning with their own stories and their own secrets.

> "One of my happiest moments...A few of us decided to walk to the village...suddenly we were surrounded by children coming home from school. They were happy, giggly, beautiful... mischievous and curious about us. We began singing a song, "Di Sini Senang." (a song taught to us by Carla and David before we left for Bali—a song that is taught to every child in Bali.) At first the kids were confused, then they burst into song with us. it was unbelievably beautiful. My heart was bursting with joy...One by one we dropped the kids at their homes, waved good-bye, and the moment was over. I felt happier than I have in a long time."[25]

Being near the village of Sidemen at the Retreat Center seemed to open one's heart to all of life. Heaven and earth were one there, and I was never quite sure which one of the two I was exploring.

Also at Nirarta was a little dog named Honey who ran up and down and all around, making sure no stranger entered the compound without the handshake of his master or mistress. He was a naughty dog, who often tried to seduce the visitors into letting him enter their rooms, where he might find a soft spot to curl up and sleep.

Honey was about the size of a fox terrier, although his breed was non-descript. He wore a coat of honey-brown fur, his little ears flopped like silky petals and wiggled when he ran about. He had an overbite that said,"I am not who you think I am."

The little dog often tried to sneak into the meditation center when we were there. Honey had a little basket just outside the glass doors where he was to sleep during meditation. Peter did not always remember to close the glass door and Honey often wriggled in and lay at the toes of one of us meditating. He was able to sneak in unseen because all of us had our eyes closed.

Peter, however, miraculously often heard Honey's belly rubbing on the wood and would bellow, "Honey! Basket." Honey would slink to his basket, and we returned to our stillness.

Peter was experienced in teaching meditation. He had been practicing transcendental meditation for twenty years guided by his teacher Maharishi Mahis Yogi. Peter encouraged all of us who were not practiced in meditation to just sit in silence and listen.

The octagonal building had an exquisite roof that soared twenty-five feet upward giving a cathedral-like feeling to the structure. The roof was a traditional bamboo roof with thatch and bamboo tightly woven to form a conical ceiling adored by the geckos. There was always one gecko, whom no one ever saw, who made his home in the ceiling.

At night while we all slept, the gecko relieved itself right in the middle of the meditation center, the same spot every night. Peter cleaned the poop each morning and in its place, he set down an offering of incense, holy water, and colorful flowers on a wide circular plate that rested atop a pedestal. This offering sat on the magnificent floor, fifty feet in diameter, spread out in a swath of soft, polished wood.

Sidemen (near Nirarta). Students receiving blessings from the wife of the high priest.

Most of the eight walls were glass so that wherever you sat during meditation you could look out and see, embraced by light or rain, a dense green that was luminous. Everywhere flowers bloomed. Only in heavy rain were we forsaken by a chorus of birdsong.

Our meditation lasted forty-five minutes. Peter sat in front, facing all of us. Just behind his head was an octagonal stained glass window, blue as the sky and reflecting a feeling of spaciousness that always came as one entered that space. The wooden floor, soft like the petals of the lotus bloom, welcomed our bare feet, and the incense invited us to settle softly into being.

Peter asked us to be aware of any questions that were arising and asked us to be aware of the moment of "not knowing" that arises just before a question. He invited us to stay with that feeling of not knowing and hold it with curiosity. Then he said, "Allow yourself to slow down, drop all agendas except for just being with whatever surfaces."

It was also here in this same meditation space where Peter, David, and I sat with the students, where we welcomed them, and where Peter spoke about the place and how it came to be. The three of us nudged the students, each in our own way, to share what they were feeling about being in these new surroundings. We did not know what awakenings might occur in the next few days, what sorrows might pierce the evening, what outbursts of joy might perfume our wild, shared space. But the students were relaxed and basking in the pleasure of just being together.

> "Each of us began to talk about our feelings and our lives. It wasn't a typical conversation that you would have with a group of strangers who you hardly knew, but it was heart-felt and genuine. I felt as though I could say anything and wouldn't be judged for how I felt or what I was saying. I was so relieved to be able to be accepted by my peers without trying to impress them… all I had to do was be myself and connect with them. It was comforting to hear others feel the same way I did." [26]

> "I became aware of how close you can become to people by simply being around them."[27]

Our group was changing. Every day it was becoming more alive. There was a readiness to dive deeper, explore more fully the bigger ideas. Here a student considers a deeper dive.

"Peter talked about the importance of giving oneself permission to not know what is going on...[he] sometimes used phrases that opened up new dimensions of thought for me..."creativity comes from no-thing.," he said..."The absence of thought allows for a full expression of creativity..."[28]

A day of silence and self-reflection was planned for the students, a day mirroring the Balinese New Year, *Nyepi*. On this day in Bali, people stay at home with their families, eat delicious food prepared the day before, take a nap, talk quietly with one another, and keep the electricity shut off. Activity screeches to a halt.

Tjokorda Rai works with one of the group while Peter helps with translation.

The streets are silent. There are no planes in the sky. Around 4:00 in the afternoon people go to the entrance of their homes, to the family gate, and peep out at the completely silent streets.

Once we went with Aji and Ibu to the gate on Nyepi and peeped out. It was an eerie feeling. I felt like I was in a science fiction movie and the end of the world was coming. I am grateful, however, to have experienced Nyepi. Now it was important for Peter, David, and me to give our students a small taste of this experience of silence. They were to remain silent during the entire afternoon. We asked them not to write or read. Here the students share their discoveries:

"Silence was a weird thing for me in my Western life. If I was with someone and things got silent, I would feel awkward and as if they thought I was uninteresting. I did not realize that silence is needed. Space does not always need to be filled with words, conversation, and replies...I am finding comfort in silence. Everything that I feel does not need to be expressed...It can be felt."[29]

Nirarta. Putri Dayu showing our friend how to make a small offering.

"At first I found my mind looking for things "to do" but after awhile, I just sat in the stillness. I felt like a child exploring the world for the first time."[30]

"A thunderstorm rolled in. I could feel the air pressure dropping, calming my body. I could hear the rain falling against the roof and windows, relaxing my thoughts and keeping my focus on the present moment."[31]

"I was watching the insects at work in the rain...the ants...the spiders the preying mantises ... all this activity was interconnected. At the university...we live indoors in small rooms... There I feel separate from nature and from my fellow students... In Bali, families and gardens live together."[32]

"…most of us girls played in the river, exploring the rocks, and letting ourselves drift in the current… a living metaphor for the entire trip."[33]

It was such a pleasure for David, Peter, and me to meet with the group again after their experience of silence. We had no real agenda other than to listen. The students were relaxed and eager to share. They, too, were alert and listening to one another beautifully.

"I was sitting listening to everyone share personal experiences…I was amazed at how strong a connection we had, how strong the energy was within the room and between us. I felt an enormous sense of gratitude and love for this amazing group who gave me so many things I thought I had lost…. A sense of belonging, safety, and a feeling of being a part of something much bigger than myself."[34]

There were no papers to write, no meals to prepare, no places to go. We could rest and listen to one another. Nirarta has always been a place where visitors come to understand how the world works—underneath ideologies, interpretations, and belief systems.

We were exploring together.

Upper Left: Nirarta, David with "Manghku" in the background attending to a small offering. **Upper Right:** A student enjoying a quiet moment with the mask dancer who had been entertaining us. **Below:** After blessings at the griya (home) of the high priest.

Nirarta. Prof. Suryani, Dr. Cokorda Bagus Jaya Lesmana, "Yaya,"
David, Peter, myself, and the students

12

"Your Own Experience is Your Greatest Teacher."
"Your Healing is Up to You."
"Stop Complaining."

Dr. Luh Ketut Suryani at Nirarta

David, Peter, and I met Suryani and her son Yaya at the head of the stone stairway. As we all walked down to the dining area overlooking the river where breakfast was being prepared, a few students asked to join her at a table set for eight.

She began chatting with the students, loving every minute of being the center of attention. A discussion emerged about "the things that scare us," i.e., spiders, lightning, big waves, long, fat snakes, scorpions. She started with a joke. "I speak Balinese English," she said. Then she said, "I scare of cockroaches," and burst into laughter. She continued by describing how the sound of the cockroaches scrambling about in walls and under floorboards really terrified her.

We were all laughing now, and the discussion shifted to the topic of food. One of the students asked, "Suryani, you have been to the United States. What food did you like while you were visiting?"

Without hesitation, she laughed and said, "Reese's Peanut Butter Cups." Now she had them. She was funny, approachable, and meeting them right where they were.

The circle we formed in the meditation center felt cozy when Suryani began talking about her family, her husband, Cok Ahlit, and how they had made a family of six sons. Suryani was never really separate from her family. In fact her son Cok Yaya was by her side much of the time in those days. He was a budding psychiatrist in his own right, brilliant, autonomous and strong.

Wherever she was, when Suryani was leading throngs of people in meditation or if she was speaking at an opening ceremony at Udyana University, some of her family were always with her. On occasion, she invited David and me to join her entourage. What I often noticed was that when she began to speak to the people, the gathering itself started to feel like one large family.

The students wanted to know more about her work, the challenges in her country. When she listened to their questions, I had the sense that she was listening to what they were asking and to what they were *not* asking.

Before she talked to a group, I never had any idea of what she would say. David, Peter, Suryani, and I reviewed several possible topics beforehand, but rarely did she speak of these things. Or, if she did, she had her own compelling twist. I always felt like she was being directed from some place deep within herself.

As she led us in experiential exercises, we were entering deeper waters. The ambiguity, the not knowing about what was coming next, did not feel so threatening now. Instead, the environment felt safe, even cozy, under the roof of this bamboo chapel where the ever–present gecko lurked overhead. Suryani started by saying, "Your own experience is your greatest teacher," and went on to say that meditation is how we learn to listen deeply to our own experience.

"I have found…that listening to my own experience is the key to reaching true understanding of myself and of life itself."[35]

As a teenager, Suryani was called by a goddess to become a healer. She studied with her for many months. Her experiences during that time led her to develop a meditation process that would help individuals focus and settle into their own peaceful being. She shared this process with the students:

"Suryani's guided meditation focused on the energy in each breath as we became full with energy in the inhale and released the energy in the exhale…During the meditation I was able to establish a genuine connection to the energy inherent to my being. I became the observer. When the meditation ended, I felt my own power… I felt a sense of freedom, a freedom balanced with a feeling of being completely grounded in the present moment. I felt more like myself, than ever before."[36]

"Suryani taught me that meditation is just being with what is, i.e., just being with my own experiences. I have found that meditation is one of the best anxiety medications available…She helped me understand that meditation and relaxation can guide us through any life challenge…"[37]

In working with the students, Suryani often said, "Do not use your mental (processes)." She asked them to approach a problem by "feeling" it. Emphasis was placed on focusing on the bodily sensations and the energetic actualities that were arising.

"Suryani says that westerners want to know every detail of a problem immediately, analyze it, label it… and take a quick course of action. The Balinese approach to a problem, or pain, or any situation is very different. They recognize it, then try to feel it. By meditating, taking a step back and feeling the problem out, their body and mind can better understand it. I had trouble with this approach. My first instinct has always been to think of how to stop the problem (or pain) or what the ramifications of the problem might be in the future. I have been running from the problem instead of embracing it and feeling it… I always thought my mind was a safe place. Now I realize I am often entrapped by my mind, restricted and closed off. I realize now that **how** I think about my problems can perpetuate them…How I think about the future keeps me from focusing on the present…I discovered that frantic thoughts often get in the way of my inner peace. My mind can be loud and overbearing…I am learning to separate myself from my cognitive mind, to become the observer of the mind."[38]

Suryani also addressed the topic of healing oneself. "Your own healing is up to you." She recommended that the students first begin exploring their own inner landscape before working with others. She taught them that healing happens as we uncover the hidden feelings within. As we gently locate a part of ourselves that we never knew was there, we face our pain and touch it with a kind, comprehensive embrace. As the students deepened their ability to listen to their own experiences, they learned to heal themselves:

"In one of her exercises, Suryani lead me on a journey to my past, to feel the pain of my past, to try to not think of it, but feel it. Deep in meditation, I released my pain, tears fell from my eyes… Why did I re-experience this pain? Why did these feelings occur? As I laid there sinking into the wood floor, the answers were clear. If the events of my life, even the hardest ones to bear, had not occurred, I would not be who I am. I would not be in this moment. I laid there thankful for my most painful feelings of the past… these feelings lead me to Bali." [39]

"I had never reached closure on the matter of my father's death. While in Nirarta I allowed myself to feel my feelings around (his) death and to live through the experience. It was a very emotional time. I felt like I opened…to a whole other part of myself…This experience was one of the most beneficial… before working with Suryani and her meditation exercise I had not been able to give attention to these emotions hidden in my past. Now I was able to express my feelings. As a result I was able to heal this pain and move on."[40]

What I have found in working with Suryani is that she listens to the story of the person, affirms it in its entirety—including the complaining aspect of it. Then she challenges the necessity of the person continuing to complain. She illuminates the fact that complaining is a belief that "I am a victim." It is a "poor me" posture that entraps individuals in their own mind.

Instead, she suggests we ask, "What must we do?" as if we want to explore options, as if we are walking in an open field. Again, she invites the person to do this by noticing sensations in the body, feeling the energy of the situation. She highlights the reality that incessant complaining only embeds a sense of helplessness in the human psyche. Acceptance of things the way they are presents a full field of possibility for adaptation.

When it was time for Suryani and her entourage to go, she left the students with this: "Do what you like to do!" She encouraged the students to listen deeply to themselves and not just to their thinking minds. She invited them to listen to the things in their lives that tugged at them in a pleasant way, to listen to their passions, to listen to their hearts, and forget about what other people think they should do: "Just do what you like to do."

She was not suggesting that the students be self indulgent, but that they connect with themselves and with what they love to do before they try to be of service to others. Often her ending statement was "Life is beautiful!"

When it was time to leave Nirarta, inevitably David and I would say something like, "You all are the best group we have ever had," and we meant it. Each group was the best. As one of our students pointed out:

> "[In Bali], each day was the best, or the most unique, but as we continued to do more things, the next thing became the one thing that was best and so on. Towards the end I smiled knowing that after every day I thought, "*This was the best day; I'll hold it forever.*"[41]

13

"Do not grow old,
No matter how long you live…
Never cease to stand
Like curious children
Before the Great Mystery
Into which you were born."

—Albert Einstein—

The Children at the Gate

When babies awoke from their naps—late in the afternoon with sleepiness still in their eyes—mom or dad, grandmother or grandfather, auntie, or uncle took the baby in their arms to the gate, the entrance to the family compound. There the baby could look out and see the narrow neighborhood street now buzzing with activity.

With wide eyes, the baby watched the teenagers zoom by on their motorbikes, their bright helmets gleaming in the sun. Rockstars! Neighbors might stop by for a moment of delight, knowing that if they looked into the baby's eyes, they would see a shining light, and, possibly the spirit of an ancestor.

I, too, liked to stop and see the babies, except sometimes my white skin frightened them. I remember a story told about Margaret Mead, the famous anthropologist who did research in Bali in the 1930s, where she describes how the children in the village where she was working were sometimes terrified by her. Her white skin reminded them of a witch in Balinese cosmology named Rangda who also had a white face.[42]

Not wanting to be mistaken for Rangda, I often tended to keep a distance, letting everyone adjust to my whiteness. The villagers could feel my energy, my good intentions, so I never had to explain myself.

Up and down the street, the babies were being presented to the village. For the babies, this was a brand new world to view, one with bicycles, people on foot carrying offerings, little children racing to the ice cream cart, and dogs trotting along with serious faces as if to say, "I know exactly where I am going."

Every day the parents brought the children here. This was village life, and David and I hoped to bring our granddaughters to the gate to see this village and this new world of Bali.

It was arranged for the entire family to come to Bali: my son, Adam, his wife Laura, and their two daughters, Carlena, then eleven years old, and Mollie nine years old. My granddaughters were not babies, but we still wanted to take them to the gate to see this world of Bali very different from their own.

They arrived in Bali at Segara Village, an elegant, yet casual hotel on Sanur Beach, owned by a friend of Suryani's, and a perfect place for them to rest. On the second evening of our stay, our friend Yuni, her husband Gede, and her young sons Adik and Agus, joined us there on the beach where the almond trees grew forever along the water's edge. Towards evening, tables and chairs were placed around these magnificent trees and positioned so that those dining had a clear view

Carlena, Laura, Adam, and Mollie

Dr. Sriyuni, "Yuni," with our granddaughters

of the stage that magically appeared just around sunset. Yuni carried two tiny baskets of flowers, one for Mollie and one for Carlena. The girls dressed for dinner in fresh summer frocks, their faces already tanned by the Bali sun and received the tiny baskets from Yuni. They held them delicately until we all sat down to eat. The girls placed the tiny baskets above the spots where their plates would be placed.

We settled into this cozy setting and waited to be served chicken satay with peanut sauce, spicy green beans, and rice. We all ate heartily and were feeling the glow that comes after hours of swimming in the tropical sun. The sunset was brief, as it always is in the tropics, and brought with it cooler air.

Darkness came quickly. Just as we finished eating, torches were lit, their flames lighting up the stage. As the orchestra, a gamelan, tabla, and Balinese flute began to play, a stream of radiance flooded the stage, as little girls, crowned in gold and wearing crimson and gold sarongs and sashes, carried tiny baskets of flowers and moved with the rhythmic sounds of the gamelan with perfect synchronicity. Towards the end of their performance, the dancers, their little heads swaying from side to side, swished their way to the edge of the stage where they flung—quickly, wildly, like magic—hundreds of marigold petals from their tiny baskets into the crowd. Then they circled round, formed a single line and left the stage in much the same way as they had come.

Yuni knew that Carlena and Mollie were dancers, that their mother owned a dance studio in America and that, like the little dancers on the stage, they had been dancing since they were toddlers. Yuni knew the girls would enjoy the little dancers, and she knew, too, that both of them would understand now why they had been given flower baskets exactly like the ones carried by the dancers on the stage. Yuni had taken Carlena and Mollie to the gate and introduced them to the world of Balinese dance.

When the dancing was finished, we sat for a while on the beach, shedding our sandals and letting our toes wriggle in the sand, all the while thinking about the young dancers with the gold crowns and the little baskets of flowers. In the background, the waves were lapping on the shore, and the sky was black and filled with stars. So much beauty in one place left us feeling like we wanted to be still for a moment and let the evening soak into our bones. We would be leaving this place the next day, but for that moment, everything was perfect. It seemed we could stay forever in this spot. We would bask in the fullness of it all for just a few more minutes.

Aji and Ibu were ready for us when we arrived the next day. The space that served as a classroom for our students was now transformed into a tiny dance studio. The long low table had been removed, the large gingham pillows put to the side. The space, still held by Aji's paintings, was ready for the dancers.

We were waiting now for a famous Balinese dancer and teacher to arrive. Carlena and Mollie and Putu, a young neighbor girl, were alert as Ibu began to prepare them. She dressed the three in the traditional dance garments—sarong, fitted blouse, and sash. Mollie and Carlena were eager to have the traditional dance attire worn precisely as it needed to be worn and to have their hair tied back properly, just as the Balinese girls tied their hair when they danced. This time the children were taken to the gate to be shown how to dance *legong*. The girls welcomed Ibu's thorough inspection. They were ready to meet this new world.

When the beautiful Balinese dancer arrived, we found that she had the posture and gracefulness of a princess and the clarity and strength of a serious task master. As she stood before the dancers, she explained that in Bali, dancing positions were learned by observing and imitating the teacher, something familiar to Carlena and Mollie.

99

Putu was placed in the center, with Mollie and Carlena behind, one on each side of Putu. With this configuration, Carlena and Mollie could watch both their teacher and Putu from the back. Feet, legs, arms, hands, and neck were to be observed simultaneously. While the recorded gamelan music played, the teacher led the way through one smoothly flowing posture after another.

Every movement was new territory for Carlena and Mollie. There were starts and stops and shy laughter in between. Ibu moved into position beside Carlena, then beside Mollie, so that she could correct an arm position or tap a shoulder to release the tension. The teacher praised Carlena and Mollie's ability to concentrate. And, she was impressed by their commitment to follow Balinese traditional dance to the letter.

All the while, Ibu stayed close by. Laura, mother of Carlena and Mollie, was a dancer watching the dancers. She was fascinated to discover that the foundational dance positions in legong dance were just the opposite of the foundational positions of ballet. As they danced, it was " West meeting East." But dancers are still dancers, and the joy of moving together was apparent in all of them, including the teacher. Ibu, who had been a renowned legong dancer in her youth, also enjoyed slipping into the movement of the dance.

Three generations of dancers and two completely different cultures were represented here. My granddaughters were before me, dancing the dance of this beautiful land, holding and moving their eyes, their hands, their heads, and their bodies in the positions of the goddesses of an ancient world.

Carlena and Mollie were fascinated by the movements of the fingers, eyes, head, and neck and how they were coordinated with everything else that was happening. Such movements are not common in American dance.

The dancing continued for an hour. Ibu had prepared tea and cake for all of us when the dancing was finished. As we sipped our tea, the girls had some questions for me. *Where did we sleep when we stayed with Aji and Ibu? What did we do in Bali?*

And, their teachers wanted to acknowledge the girls for how well they did at their first attempt at legong dance. This time the teacher, Ibu, and Putu took Carlena and Mollie to the gate to meet a world ancient and compelling and with all the accoutrements of fun.

It recently occurred to me that Mollie and Carlena had taken David and me to the gate as well. As little girls throughout their childhood and adolescence, they took us into *their* world of dance, always sparkling and alive with anticipation of their next dance performance. Each year, they carefully prepared us, just as Ibu had

Aji guiding my family through The Agung Rai Museum in Ubud.

prepared them. Each year, we became more and more curious about the dances. And, each year their dances were different than any of the dances we had previously seen.

I was presented with a T-shirt. Now, these T-shirts lie neatly stacked in my closet. They read, "On Broadway," "So You Think You Can Dance?" "Road Trip Across America," "Wicked Enchantment," "Who Dunnit?" "Dancing with the Decades" "Channel Surfing," "Wonderful World of Disney."

On the back of each T-shirt were the names of hundreds of courageous dancers who worked hard that year to grow beyond what they knew, to find a fresh, more expressive, more sophisticated way to dance.

David was presented with a copy of the program. When he opened the program, our granddaughters had highlighted all of their dances in PINK!

David and I were ready now. And, despite the inevitable frenzy and wild activity that filled the house before such performances, Carlena and Mollie remained kind and generous to us as we waited for the show to begin.

I was always nervous waiting for the curtain to go up. When it did, we saw tiny tip-toeing ballerinas in light pink tutus, with stockings so white they made you blink; older dancers wearing shiny dresses of silver sequins shimmying and alighting on the sounds of jazz; children tap, tap tapping their way through a Broadway melody; girls on point, dancing snowflakes, dressed in white satin costumes with puffy, long, soft crinoline skirts that flowed with each leap.

Still, my nervousness would not leave me. Like the Balinese parents at the gate, I felt somewhat protective of Mollie and Carlena. What if they made a mistake or fell or hurt themselves?

Adam and Laura, however, knew their children were precisely where they needed to be, on stage, each finding her own heart and soul, her own fear, artistry, and strength. The girls did make mistakes. And, I did see them fall and hit the stage with a thud on occasion. But Carlena and Mollie accepted these things as part of what it means to be a dancer. Sometimes tears of disappointment were shed. But, their misery never lingered.

Each year, they started from scratch. New dances were placed before them. The choreographers expected them to start from what they knew and go beyond that. Once on the ride, they had to feel their way to where their choreographer wanted them to be. Heading towards unknown territory, they always found something inside themselves to meet the challenges of whatever dance they were given.

I have seen them do this over and over again. They are still doing this. Carlena and Mollie have taken us to the gate and shown us that we can find in ourselves what is needed for the challenge and that we must surrender everything. We have to bring everything to the table if we want to experience more of who and what we are. Also, they have shown David and me that we must trust that something within us will keep nudging us on along our way as we stay open to The Great Mystery.

Part II
The Return to Bali

14
Post-Pandemic Pandemonium

Will we be welcomed in Bali? How much had things changed since the pandemic?

A young Balinese woman approached us, her hair tied back in the Balinese knot, her presentation fresh yet formal in an exquisitely tailored pale pink long skirt and long sleeve jacket. Speaking softly and with a welcoming smile, she let us know she would be our guide throughout the airport proceedings. We were on our way to the immigration desk where elderly people do not wait in long lines but instead are processed quickly and directed on to the baggage claim area. She and David and I moved together like a little family until we reached the area where the moving belts were filling up with bags popping out from behind the mysterious flapping door.

David and I spotted our monster bags. Our helper recruited three young Balinese men to fling our bags onto a cart. This group, the young woman and the three men, were strangers and yet they smiled and talked together as if they were on a walk in the park, a stroll down the beach. Their energy was light, their manner easy.

The Balinese know how to make visitors feel welcome and at ease. This crew was no exception. Our traveling family now was extended to six as we moved on to the security check area. With a nod from the officials, we were allowed to roll on into a long, narrow, passageway that opened like a mouth out into a sea of people all waiting to welcome and transport weary travelers to a favorite spot in Bali.

The young woman who was pushing my wheelchair stayed with us until our friends were spotted in the distance. Her smiles opened a pathway through the crowd, the guys followed close behind, until we were with our friends.

In that very place, we said goodbye to these lovely people. I remembered that fifteen years prior in an older air terminal, David was wheeled along in a wheelchair, having just broken his collarbone three days before. He was welcomed and cared for with the same kindness that we received on this day of our return to Bali. Some things had not changed.

Our friends, Yaya and his wife Tesna, helped us get our luggage into their car. After Yaya packed the lumpy duffle bags neatly in the trunk, Tesna slowly and calmly maneuvered the car through the parking garage, a cavern of darkness and complicated traffic patterns. No signs were visible and, in this tangle of turns, we finally saw the light of day and the street that would lead us to the overpass straight to the main road. We were excited now as we always were when we arrived in Bali. Our fatigue had vanished. In a short time, we would be in Tebesaya—or so we thought.

"What is all this traffic, Tesna?" I asked. As she was looking about for a way to exit the main road, she explained that bumper to bumper traffic was common now. "Finding a side road to get from one place to another is critical if we want to keep moving," she said.

She took us on side roads where nothing looked familiar. *Was this the same Bali we remembered?* Apparently during the pandemic, the traffic was sparse. But now since the government had opened the airport to the rest of the world, people were flooding into Bali, renting cars and motorbikes, and, in turn, overwhelming the motorways. Local news reported tens of thousands of visitors had entered Bali in the past two months. Some were escaping war, others were seeking tourist visas. And still others hoped to attain business visas and make Bali their home. All this activity came at the end of a three year period in which the entire world was quarantined. Now people were traveling again, and we were sitting in the middle of the masses on the move.

Over the centuries, Bali has accommodated all kinds of visitors: Hindus came from Java in the 13th century, the results of which meant that Balinese-Hinduism became the primary religion of the island. In 1906, the Dutch arrived and massacred hundreds of noblemen and took control of the island. During World War II, the Japanese occupied the island and were claimed to be even more harsh than the Dutch. It was 1949 before Bali's independence—along with Indonesia's—was declared by the Netherlands.

Since then, there have been trying times. Political conflict from 1963-65 left 500,000 Indonesians killed, 80,000 of which were Balinese. In the 1970s, tourists started to reappear in Bali in larger numbers. Then there was an economic crisis in the late 1990s, and bombings by militant Islamists in both 2002 and 2005 killed hundreds of people, the majority of which were tourists. As a result, tourism was severely reduced, which in turn prompted severe economic hardship.

Since 2006, the tourist numbers in Bali have grown by leaps and bounds. In 2018, there were two million visitors to the island, more than half the entire population of Bali. Most recently in the glossy travel magazines and in the more popular travel websites, Bali has been depicted as "The Resort Island," a description that is thoughtless and dismissive of the Balinese people and their culture.

Bali is home to three-and-a-half-million people. The ancestors of these people have lived here for thousands of years. People continue to move on and off the island, millions every year. Some of these millions are tourists and return home refreshed. Others will attempt to start businesses and establish themselves on the island in a way that is to their own liking—with little regard for the Balinese culture or for the laws of the land.

This kind of aggression has gone on for centuries and on every continent. As an American, I am not proud of the fact that my ancestors arrived on a land that is now known as the United States of America and took everything they wanted, leaving Native Americans, who had been living on that land for thousands of years, with few resources.

On our return visit to Bali, when we needed transportation, our routine was to walk to the end of the street, Jalan Sukma Kesuma, and find a driver. Our driver told us that within the last six months, many businesses had been established in Bali, businesses that endanger Balinese jobs. He gave us an example of a visitor who bought several hundred motorbikes to establish a motorbike rental business, a lucrative business that has always been owned and managed by Balinese. We heard another story of yet another visitor who leased land in a quiet village on the outskirts of Ubud and opened a discotheque. Where there once were harvests throughout the year, now there was night life. Other visitors have started surfing and snorkeling businesses.

The question arises, "Can the Balinese government enforce the laws in place to protect Balinese land and Balinese businesses?" That would mean that the process of attaining a business identification card and the number of foreigners attaining such cards would need to be carefully monitored.

Like the rest of the world, Bali is struggling to manage the flow of people coming in and going out of their land. Visitors have always been welcomed by the Balinese people. I suspect that will always be true but recent offenses committed by visitors from all over the world, e.g., defacing the sacred banyan trees, and displaying nakedness and behaviors offensive to the Balinese people and their culture, have necessitated action on the part of Balinese officials. Over one hundred offenders have been deported in recent months.

The stress on the Balinese is real and has intensified these last three years. Nevertheless, the Balinese people are strong and intelligent people who plan to hold this invasion of marauders at bay.

While sitting in a traffic jam with Suryani's son, Wawan, I asked, "Do you think Bali's culture will be lost in this onslaught of globalization?"

This intelligent man, tough, and with a great sense of humor, replied with a smile. "No, of course not. But we Balinese must be willing to change. We must be modern, awake, and knowledgeable of the latest innovations." We continued to talk about the state of affairs on the island, his family joining into the conversation.

I felt hopeful about Bali's future after being with Wawan and his family. As one of the island's leaders, along with many other strong Balinese leaders on the island, he will see to it that the Balinese people are equipped with what they need to engage in this modern world, and, at the same time, see to it that the Balinese people stay firmly embedded in what is the essence of their beloved culture.

On several occasions, I heard Wawan's mother, Professor Suryani say so eloquently, "It is our pleasure to have you as our guests. Enjoy the beauty here. Refresh yourselves. Then go home."

15

From Heart to Hardware and Back Again

The staff was waiting for us as our driver parked the car across the street from the entrance to our little hotel. The young men quickly wrestled our bags from the car and headed down the long, narrow pathway that led to our place on the edge of the rainforest near the river. We were just a few hundred feet from "Hidden," our place away from traffic, close to friends, and near little shops and restaurants.

On either side of this pathway were Balinese homes, their exterior stone walls sprouting ferns and flowers to guide the way. Just before we started down the path, a little girl, dressed in a yellow dress with small pink flowers dancing on her bodice, stood under the large frangipani tree in front of her home. Her large dark eyes invited us to come and see her puppy.

These two were perfectly matched—their energy fresh, their playfulness soft as the puppy's white fur. The world was theirs, and they explored it together. I blurted out awkwardly, "*Cantik sekali,*" meaning "very beautiful." The little girl smiled and in a flash turned to face us directly so as to demonstrate how she could guide the puppy with the dog leash. The tiny puppy followed her lead, his little tail and ears pointed straight up to the clear blue sky.

The dog was Kintamani, a heritage to be proud of if you are a dog in Bali. "*Siapa nama mu?*" I asked. "What is your name?"

"Putu," she said. We saw her often during our two-month stay in Tebesaya, always with her puppy, always smiling, and each time demonstrating the puppy's prowess.

When we continued down the pathway arriving at the reception area, our bags had already been taken to our rooms and cool drinks prepared to welcome us. This energetic staff was present twenty-four hours a day always with one young man at the desk. I had brought them gifts from the Green Mountain State: T-shirts and chocolate. They were delighted. This was our home now for the next two months.

Just outside our bungalow to the left, a small swimming pool tucked into the little gardens provided visitors a quick dip or an hour of sizzling in the sun. David and I preferred to luxuriate in the lounge chairs shaded by umbrellas and to look out into the majestic trees that seemed to take me by the hand.

On the far side of the pool was a bamboo wall five feet high. On top sat eleven ducks fussing with each other and looking as if they might flutter away—had they not been carved in stone. At the corner of the pool nearest the forest sat a frog two-and-a-half-feet high. He, too, was stone and covered in moss. The deep stillness of these stone creatures settled me, and I found myself putting my book aside and just staring into space. In this moment, nothing had to change.

On our very first trip to Bali, while David and I were waiting to collect our bags, David was drawn to an older woman standing next to him. She had long white hair tied back in a ponytail and was dressed in khaki shirt and slacks perfect for the tropics. David's eyes softened, something that always happens when he is curious. He was feeling "the tug." I knew that when he felt that tug, he was going to act on it. He said to the lady with a smile, " Hi! My wife and I have just arrived here in Bali for the first time. Have you been to Bali before?"

"Yes," she said, "Many times."

"Oh," he said. "I wonder if you might have some advice for us."

"Of course," she said. "The most important thing to remember is to stay still and let Bali come to you."

This advice stayed with us, guiding us on every trip. And, when we brought students to the island, we shared this advice with each one of them.

Now, on this return trip, I would let Bali come to me again.

Hidden
Carla Newman Osgood

That frog is
Having fun
At the corner
Of the pool.

The ducks fight, sometimes
But the frog does not

Carved in limestone,
Porous,
Wet and cool.
Covered softly in moss
So green I have to laugh.
He merely sits.

The sun hits his face
He does not care.

Dragonflies
Red and Orange
Dart about his head.
He does not care.

For on his spot
Beneath
The breadfruit tree
He belongs to
The universe
And he is free.

We wandered out of "Hidden" with our friend, Nicky, and made our way to "The Food Court." This little restaurant shouldered the *pura dalem*, one of three of the village temples, and sat at the highest point on the street. Its veranda, open on three sides, had comfortable bamboo picnic tables scattered about.

On this perch, we sat enjoying the breeze and catching sight of the tall palm trees gently blowing in the wind just across the street. We pretended not to be bothered by the whooshing of the motor bikes as they zoomed down the newest, the smoothest, the most wonderful street in Ubud.

Everyday, we ate lunch at this restaurant at the same table with the same servers. We had scrumptious salads served really cold; sandwiches sometimes scrunchie, sometimes squishy, but always really tasty; omelets, that would make even a French person quiver; and *nasi goreng* (without chili, made especially for me). The drinks were ice cold, and we could have as much ice as we wished.

Ranti was the head server, a beautiful young woman with shiny eyes, an alert presence, and an intuitive sense of management. We learned later that she and Guspau, a young man who helped with serving, went down to the market early every morning to buy fresh greens, fresh chicken, and fresh eggs.

Because the cook worked by himself in the kitchen, and because he was quite precise, we often had to wait awhile for our food. We were not unhappy about this, however, because we knew what was coming. We referred to him as "the chef" and made sure he knew how much we enjoyed his food. He was pleased with our attention.

Ranti, Guspau, and "the chef," all three, were curious about us. *Why do these three rather large white people come to eat here everyday?*

The truth is we came because the food was delicious and because Ranti and Guspau and "the chef" pampered us. They wanted to know how long we would be staying in the village. They looked for us everyday, and, when they saw us coming from across the street, they started up the reggae music. I was reminded of days long past—it was like going to a picnic.

When I was a little girl, sometimes Mom and Dad took my brother and me on picnics. After church on Sunday, Dad—a hard core atheist most of his life—picked us up. In the trunk of the car was a basket of food Mom had prepared. The basket was filled with goodies, the treats stacked so high above the basket line that when Mom placed a tablecloth over the top, it looked like a miniature mountain, checkered in red and white.

Dad often selected the same roadside park with picnic table, a small grill, and lots of woods nearby. Mom and I set the picnic table with a tablecloth, cloth napkins, and real silverware. Dad started up the grill to roast the hotdogs and my brother Dick peeled off to explore the surrounding woods.

A small ice chest was placed on the edge of the picnic table. Inside, plunked on a bed of ice, was a cherry jello salad filled with a million tiny marshmallows, sliced red grapes, and pecans, all topped with real whipped cream. Next to the chest was a bowl as big as Chicago filled with potato chips. The hot dogs lay neatly aligned next to the chips, perfectly roasted, stuffed into buns that were perfectly toasted. Ketchup, mustard, onions, and pickles galore were spread out over the length of that table ready to be squeezed, dabbed, and dotted onto the hotdogs.

When we sat down to eat, you could feel a hum, a hum that emerged from sheer and utter contentment, the contentment of just being together. My family was moving together now, saturated in the hum, the breeze, the comfort food, and the conversation that marks a simple and precious moment forever. Such was our time with Ranti, Guspau and the "chef.

On this visit, I was looking for fabric—bright, colorful fabric with wild patterns. I was looking to buy Balinese sarongs which I would tailor into a shirt for my son, a blues harmonica player, who at times searches for shirts that vibrate with his music.

The main road through Ubud is named Jalan Raya, better known to our students as "The Beast." This road during the day, early evening, and at night was always fiercely busy with trucks, tourist buses, and motor bikes and cars driven by Balinese and tourists. To cross this street took courage, agility, and remembering to look to the RIGHT before you cross the street because the traffic drives on the LEFT side of the street. If there is anything at all to be frightened of in Bali—outside of dengue fever—it is Jalan Raya.

David and Nicky and I had a delicious supper at "The Herb Garden," which I often referred to as the "fu-fu" restaurant. It was part of a larger resort, open on all four sides and positioned in the middle of a heartbreakingly beautiful garden. The restaurant served salads that were the best I have ever had, along with fancy herbal drinks and luscious desserts.

We were satiated now from all the good food and feeling confident as we walked along Jalan Raya. This particular evening we did not have to cross "The Beast." We walked alongside it as it growled with traffic and spewed exhaust fumes, and we focused on finding a small side street where we knew a night market was taking place.

We found the entrance, walked in, and were enchanted by a semicircle of open air tents, each strung with tiny white lights. The two tents that caught my eye had hundreds of sarongs. In each of these tents were two women with their own stash.

It was towards the end of their day of selling, and they looked tired. When they saw me, however, they became alert, focused on where my eyes were landing. No one ever walks into a Night Market in Bali without the intention of buying and they were interested in what I was interested in.

My eyes fell on something perfect—ink black batik designs with hues of raspberry, scarlet, and gold Bali birds and ancient geometric patterns. The lady–of–the–stall splayed it before me. "Do you have another like this one? I asked.

"*Ma'af,*" she said, "*Sorry,* I just have one."

I needed two to make my son's shirt. The lady working with me took charge. Without hesitation, she instructed the others to search among their combined supplies to see if another sarong like the one I initially picked could be found.

A wave of searching spread over the entire area, women with heads down on a mission. After a few minutes, bedlam ensued. Three of the searchers thrust sarongs before me, nothing like what I wanted. The same woman took charge again, and bellowed "Pelan, pelan" meaning "slowly, slowly."

After a pause, I pointed to the pattern and colors I liked. The four dispersed and continued looking for what might please me. This time the ladies returned with two sarongs almost like the one I previously selected except the hues were slightly different—raspberry and burgundy rather than raspberry and red.

I shook my head. "No, that won't do." Tension hung in the air and I continued looking at the fabric.

Instantly, they all knew what that meant. I would bargain with the leader.

"How much you want to pay?" she said.

I gave her an expected rock-bottom price.

She responded dramatically. "No, no, not possible." Then she gave me a ridiculously high price.

We were off and running—back and forth, back and forth. Everyone was relaxed now. Everyone was smiling, each following the process closely. I had done this many times before in the market and only once did a man try to bully me into buying. This evening, all was well.

When I was bargaining in the markets in Bali, I learned to sense early on in the process whether the seller was going to work with me, whether she would take her time, stay relaxed, and let her sense of humor take the lead. I could feel the energy in the atmosphere, something Suryani had been training me to do. With these seasoned sellers the process of bargaining was a well known dance, energetic and fun. In this case all the ladies instinctively knew I would buy and that I had already decided on the range within which I would settle. Nicky, who along with David, was standing off to the side and watching the entire scenario, remarked at how lively the ladies were. When the price was agreed upon, I paid the lady, and she turned and divided the money equally among the four. This was a collaborative event. These ladies wanted my money, but they also wanted me to be happy. In Bali, in the final round of bartering, there must be a hum. A hum that comes from the heart.

We left Tebesaya for a few days to stay at our favorite fancy hotel on Sanur Beach. The reception area was an open air pavilion, tasteful, elegantly appointed with Balinese sculptures and weavings.

Magnificent orchids, artistically displayed on an antique marble-top table, caught my attention.

I approached the large desk and was invited to sit down across from the receptionist, who was sitting behind a computer. The focus shifted now to this hardware and the data to be received and retrieved from it.

I felt tense. *Did the computer have record of our reservations? Did I understand correctly the cost of each night? Would the WiFi- work properly?*

The receptionist was pleasant, efficient, but a little distracted by another guest who was also needing something to be retrieved from her computer. Admittedly, we, too, were somewhat preoccupied, focused on the computer. We'd planned to arrive in the early morning hours, when Wi-Fi was supposed to be excellent and bungalows and gardens were silent. By choosing this place, David and I were confident that we were making a good "hardware" choice.

The resort was owned by a Balinese family and spread over acres of land lining the beach. The gardens were magnificent, the bungalows comfortable and convenient. On this same land stood the private family compound off to the side and apart from the hotel blueprint which included four swimming pools, two restaurants, and two bars, one facing the ocean with a loud sound system and lots of space for dancing. The other bar looked something like a floating whale submerged in the middle of one of the pools. One could swim up to the bar, order a martini, sit down on a stool next to the bar, and never get out of the water.

Because this was a large hotel, administrative tasks such as the checking people in and out, maintenance of the rooms, making reservations for meals, scheduling SPA activities, snorkeling outings, and temple tours were handled by employees skillful at using a particular computer program especially designed for each activity.

When we went to breakfast, before we were seated, our names

and room numbers needed to be retrieved from the computer list. If we needed towels for the swimming, a computer list had to be checked to determine whether our previous towels, used the day before, had been returned. If we needed to change rooms because disco music pounded late into the early morning hours, data from the computer concerning room availability had to be checked. If in the evening we wanted to eat at one of the restaurants, we needed to make reservations. This data was entered on a computer and checked by the hostess when we entered the dining area in the evening. If we ordered drinks and snacks during the day, these items were charged to our room number. Again this data was entered on a computer.

This hotel was no different than any other modern day hotel of high standing. Living in a computerized world, guests expect that employees will be focused on entering and retrieving data much of the time. The staff was neither concerned about what the customer was actually experiencing, nor were they necessarily picking up on what was behind a guest's question. In other words, the staff was not tuned into a guest's tone of voice, or if the guest was smiling, or if a guest was about to collapse from exhaustion, having just come off a fifteen-hour flight.

There were so many guests and not enough staff in those post-pandemic days, and the management challenges seemed monumental. The focus was strictly on moving people in and out of the restaurants and bungalows as efficiently and swiftly as possible. The employees had been trained to be polite, to say, "Have a nice day, " and to check guest lists and room numbers obsessively. What was missing, however, was evidence that the staff was genuinely curious and interested in the customers. They were buried in data and did not have time to be curious about their guests. People streamed in by the dozens every day, and the staff set about their work much like the machines upon which they depended. No one asked, "What happens if the computer breaks down?" And no one really seemed to care.

The gardeners on the property were less dependent on computers than the inside staff, although I am sure their salaries were noted on a list on the computer along with a stream of other lists that kept hotel operations chugging along with efficiency and profitability. These gardeners worked from sunup to sundown, rarely being noticed by guests and were accustomed to never being seen. But, the trees talked to them, as did the bushes, the flowers, the grasses, the fountains—all letting the gardeners know what was needed.

One morning, I stopped to say hello to a young man raking our lawn. I made a sweeping gesture with my arm across the expanse. "You do a beautiful job here. Thank you," I said. "Bagus sekali, terimah kasih banyak."

His eyes widened, he smiled brightly and replied. "Sama, sama." "You are welcome."

A small bale stood near the stone wall that defined the family compound. Stretched out on its large couch, we had a partial view of the compound and the family temple within. Tiers of tiny roofs towered here and there pointed to the heavens and hovered above sacred spaces as if to hold God's presence there for all eternity. We spent hours here near this silent place, talking and snoozing and pretending to be young again. David referred to this spot as "his office" and in the early morning hours, when only the gardeners were moving about, he worked with his clients, 12,000 miles away.

Sometimes a sweet spot was born when heart and hardware converged. For example, computers enabled us to continue our work with our clients while enjoying Bali. We also knew, however, that if we spent too much time on the computer, we would not be experiencing Bali—our time in Bali could be blurred by computer fret and our sense of what we were about could get muddled. Fortunately, our hearts usually told us when it was time to sink back into just being in Bali.

In this beautiful bale facing east stood a banyan tree hundreds of years old, dripping its roots to the earth, forming many other smaller banyan trees. As you gazed upon the tree from a distance, the mother and babies appeared as one tree. I liked to walk around that massive tree keeping my gaze upward, just listening.

The tree beckoned those who were interested. Once the tree had your attention, the tree was silent. And silence begat silence. Without that tree, I might not have remembered that silence was an option. The tree held me in that space, held me in a silence that comforted me, left me feeling like that frog, spacious and free. I spent most of my time at the resort near that tree.

On the other side of the banyan tree was an abandoned cottage. Years before, it had served as a gift shop and tiny pharmacy. At that time the shop proudly displayed beautiful hand-crafted pieces to be worn or gazed upon. Now the cottage was empty. It stood like a scarlet ibis among the trees, its bright red color marking a time when aesthetics took precedence over efficiency and productivity. I always felt its mystery when I passed, and I wondered if other guests did as well. There was a sense of melancholy that set in if I came close to the cottage. Like the tree, the cottage seemed to want to speak to me. "Stay with me. I am a tabernacle of love and you can feel that if you will just stand still." *What will happen if the owners decide to tear that old building down?* I thought.

Just outside the boundaries of our hotel, down a cobbled bike path that followed the shoreline, we found a marvelous tiny outdoor warung (restaurant). The tables were set out under the almond trees that lie close to the lapping waves and the bobbing fishing boats.

The little restaurant had two dogs, one we named Blackie, First-in-Command, and Yellow Dog who took his orders from Chief Blackie. We remembered the alpha dog from our visit here a few years before. His fur was scruffier now, his belly more plump.

Blackie and Yellow Dog were on constant patrol circling the outside perimeter of the little restaurant making sure no stray fellows from the beach came too close to this hallowed ground. This place was busy at times, but the servers were as skillful and relaxed as people are when they know exactly what they are doing. We never gave our room number, nor were our names searched for on a list. We simply gave our choices, and our server went off to tell the cook. Even on days when all the tables were filled, the servers never forgot to check back within minutes after serving our food to see if all was to our liking. They just were not distracted by the busy-ness, and, no customer was ever hurried there. Soon hamburgers, avocado lassies, and french fries were served.

Sometimes in Bali, you just have to have a hamburger. This is one of my favorite places in the world because the food is always so good and the atmosphere is friendly and relaxed. People come from all over the world to this tiny place. Rarely did I hear English spoken, although when we ordered, we spoke in English, as did the servers. The dogs and the staff, the trees and the boats, and the sun and the rain all played together to leave me feeling right at home, a real indicator of whether an environment is dominated by heart or hardware. I find it difficult to feel at home in a computerized setting, which seems reasonable to me in that a computer is a machine, and I am not.

David and I rose early to catch the sunrise. The air was heavy and the clouds moved in. We sat with our coffee on the beach in our favorite lounge chairs that allow even old people to get up and down with ease. Two large white Kintamani dogs came to join us. They plopped down at our feet and stayed with us until we went to breakfast. In Bali, one often feels the presence of companions. That day, our companions were two very friendly white dogs.

On another occasion, I was sitting by myself with hundreds of Balinese women, all of us wearing adat and watching a cremation, the fire destroying the last bits of a human being and releasing the spirit to its journey home. I sat a distance from the women, not wanting to disturb them in any way.

Every time I was in a situation like this, the women started scooting towards me in small increments. Little by little on all sides, I felt the women moving in closer and closer. I later named this movement "scooching." It was so subtle, at first, I thought I was imagining it. When the scooching was completed, I felt a Balinese sister on either side of me, their shoulders touching my shoulders, the outsides of their thighs touching my thighs. We were a sea of sisters.

Suddenly, I was transported in time to a beach at a small lake in Michigan. The sun was hot. My mom, Mary, and her sisters, Catherine, Margaret, and Helen, were all sitting together in the shade under a tiny tree, scooching.

David and I were sitting in our favorite spot in the gardens when members of the family that owned the hotel strolled past pushing their mother, the matriarch of the family, in a wheelchair. She was meticulously dressed in adat. The wheelchair indicated that her legs were wobbly, but the shine in her eyes could be seen from a hundred feet away. When her eyes met ours, she waved and smiled as if to say, "Welcome to our home. Hope you are having a wonderful time."

I thought to myself, "*This is a woman who has done a great deal of scooching in her day. This is not a women who is going to allow that scarlet cottage to be torn down.*"

16

It Was as if We Never Left

It was as if we'd never left. In Tebesaya, the trees have been chopped down along the street, the dirt roads have been paved so that now they lie like hotplates in the sun, the main street is inundated with endless new shops. Yet, still, there was a sense of something remaining in place, a timeless presence that continued to make us feel right at home.

Friends and family spread out across the compound like a colorful blanket the day we celebrated Aji's eightieth birthday. The heat of morning herded us into shady spots where we waited for the speeches to start.

Years had passed since we had seen these beautiful faces, some of whom I saw first when they were little boys. I remembered how it felt to hold them on my lap. A daughter's face stood out that morning. She spotted a leaf on Aji's chest and with a tenderness I seldom see, she brushed it to the ground.

This is how it is in the families in Tebesaya. Hardly ever do you hear a baby cry, and never do you hear parents screaming at their children.

Throughout my life, I have been aware of timeless presence. Once when my cousins and I gathered at the funeral parlor, we waited for the rosary to begin. The prayers rattled on in clumps of ten. When everything settled into silence, my brother, Dick, the eldest of the cousins and leader of our tribe, swooped in. He had us form a circle where before we prayed in rows of four.

Time rolled back. We were kids again telling stories that tied us to my mother, her sense of humor, her mischief, and her love. It was as if she never left us.

On another occasion, when I was in the Peace Corps, David invited me to visit him. I traveled west along the coast in a vessel I learned to love and hate. The "Lady Northcote" took me to a settlement at the mouth of a river whose name I've never known. David was there to greet me and we headed off to a place where dreams were made. There was no time, although we watched the pigs eat grapefruit rind, perused the jars of pickled snakes in the corner of the living room, walked the road lined with rubber trees and drank sweet tea at noontime.

Time has rolled forward since then. David and I have morphed into full-fledged adults. Sixty years have passed, and, still, when I am doing something apart from him, when I return from wherever I have been, it is as if I never left him.

In Bali, David and I sat with our students every day. We all listened as if everything would be revealed. Like a family at the dinner table, we waited to hear the day's reports of who and what we saw and heard and what we felt. A toddler splashed in a plastic tub too small for mom to give him a proper scrub. A string of ladies streamed down the road, a tower of offerings on their heads. A dragonfly, orange, fluttered in place just long enough for two of us to see her. Strange memories ascended, sharp and sweet, yanked to the surface by who knows what. It was safe to hold them here to see if they might speak.

Every talent of our being was recruited, every skill engaged. The spirits of our teachers from the past lingered by our side.

When our group returned to Vermont, we gathered for our final meeting. David and I set a circle of chairs in our living room. Near the woodstove, coats hung on a rack, soggy with snow, waiting to be dried by the heat. We spoke that evening knowing that we belonged precisely where we were. We were warmed by our closeness, and surprised to feel as if we had never left one another.

We learned in Bali that we never know when we will be touched by love. But, sometimes, when we return from wherever we have been, we find again that love we once found, and it is as if we never left.

Made Warsaw, traditional Balinese body worker, preparing a penjor for a village ceremony.

17

There is No Other Way

"Made took my bag from my hands as if he thought I was crazy to even consider carrying it myself. I was stunned at this gesture and when we reached the taxi, I was hit with an overwhelming wave of emotions. I'd heard rumors that in Bali hugs were reserved for only the closest friends and family, but Made must have sensed that I was looking for one…I looked him in the eye, thanked him several times…Suddenly he opened his arms for an embrace and drew me in…I had to choke my tears back and get into the car before I cried my eyes out in front of everyone…Made Warsa's impact on me was indescribable…I will forever remember the kindness bestowed upon me by him and his family."[43]

The students are hyper now as they face the last hours of their stay in Bali; in the garden Ibu Wati and her daughter, Cadek, along with our students are making decorations, palm leaf sculptures that hang like long, feathery swords attached to lines of string that form a canopy between the garden wall and the veranda. Peter will dance his silly dance tonight, one in which he pretends to dance perfectly with the Balinese dancer. The rest of us will follow. Our Balinese friends will laugh at us unmercifully. Darkness is coming now, the soft lights allow us to continue to see the garden wall, alive with blossoms and plants, the weightless swords moving slightly with the breeze. Ibu Wati, our dear friend, and mother of us all, is putting the final touches on the decorations.

> "The final ceremony at our compound was filled with joy, tears, laughter, dancing, and ceremony-everything that Bali represents to me. We began with the agni holtra, the fire ceremony...The moment that we threw our slips of paper into the fire was such a (powerful) culmination of the trip...I wrote on my piece of paper that I wanted to bring love and healing to the world, and as I watched it burn and slowly turn to ash and float into the air this feeling of self-assuredness washed over me. I had never felt so sure of my purpose in my life than in that moment. Under the full moon with a beautiful group surrounding me, with the fire burning close to my face, the fragrant smells of the flowers and the incense, the chants of the priests, the soft touch of Mila's tiny hand on my knee. That was Bali...It was surrender to sensation, to life, the strength of not only (being with) that which was not familiar, but delighting in it. Delighting in difference."[44]

While writing this, I learned that Ibu Wati has died. Many of our friends both in Bali and the States are growing old. All of us slog through our days with aches and pains. We are at the end of our lives—not the beginning, not the middle. I cling to the railing now when I go upstairs. I eat too much of David's delicious stew and my digestive system is screaming for the rest of the week. I can never find my glasses, and when I get out of a chair, I slap and rub my lower spine to wake the sleepy circulation there and relieve the stab of arthritis.

Mama and Bapak, a couple of our older friends in Bali, recently bought two black stone statues and placed them at the entrance of their compound. Chubby and charming, the statues depict an older couple grinning from ear to ear, adorned with gold jewelry, dressed to set out for the temple and chiseled to hold forever a posture of joy.

My friends have reminded me to be happy in my old age. Balinese often meet life this way, with smiles natural as the wind blowing or the rain falling. David and I wonder if the Balinese smiles will continue to saturate the island as the computer and the cell phone, the tools of the corporate world, take center stage. In this dance between old and new, how shall we move? Will we choreograph our own dance, or will we follow the dance of the corporate world, robotic and rigid, focused exclusively on profit and proficiency?

We do not know if we will ever return to Bali. The world is at war in many places on the planet. And, a question hangs in the balance. *Will we continue to find within ourselves what the Balinese people wanted us to embrace?*

Like diving deep into the ocean, exploring Bali has challenged David and me and our students to follow our curiosity and feel the freedom of that choice. Our motivation came from within ourselves. Our own flutter kicks propelled us.

But, at times we needed a torch to see. When Aji walked with us through the temple at Odalan, when Suryani stood with us to watch the little dancing angels, when Peter guided us in meditation on the soft wood floor, they each lit a torch and handed it to us. Ibu dressed me in adat. Ibu Wati carefully attended to the details of our final celebration. Nyoman Sujana tirelessly facilitated with his translations and guidance when we attended ceremonies and events. Aji planned creative activities for the children in the village and invited our students to participate. Professor Suryani taught our students to listen deeply to their own experience and trust it completely. Suryani's son, Yaya, and his wife, Tesna, their family, Cok Laksmi, Cok Gita, Cok Bagus, Cok Raja and our family shared so many hours together talking about what was most important to us, at times swimming until we were exhausted and eating grilled seafood on the beach at Jimberan until we were stuffed. We watched the children grow so rapidly it took our breath away.

So many Balinese people helped us along the way. We worked together, Balinese and Americans, side by side, the Balinese often taking the lead, David and I clarifying the focus of the course. Conflicts arose between students, between students and teachers, between Balinese and Americans, but not many. And, we had a way of sitting with our differences. Some days we laughed all day long. Some days were more somber. We took care of ourselves and stayed open to different ways of doing things. It was fun!

> "From day one our group formed a team and we were all there for each other the whole two weeks …I have never seen a group work so well together so fast. I will forever keep the lessons learned in Bali close to my heart."[45]

> "In embracing difference and surrendering to new experience without judgment of myself or others I stepped out of my American mind and learned more about myself and about the world…I moved alongside the Balinese with ease, smelling what they smelled, eating what they ate, feeling some of what they felt; moving with what was different between us and elating in the sameness, delighting in the true essence of the human experience, which is love, the kind of love that breathes and breeds and permeates, the love that we so often forget in America, the love for ourselves, and the love for each other, the love that lies coiled deep inside of our hearts that is so rarely accessed, the love that only a place like Bali can unearth and foster. Bali, in all that it was for me and all that it will continue to be, is love."[46]

Deep within the hearts of the Balinese people, a prayer bell is continuously ringing, reminding the people to work together as One, for there is no other way.

May all the people of the planet listen carefully for the ringing of this bell and heed its message—with a skip and a jump—welcoming the differences along the way.

Left: David with students at the final celebration. **Upper Right:** Students participating in a ceremony, agnihotra, at the final celebration. **Lower Right:** "Ahlit" playing the gamelan for our final celebration.

L-R: "Mama," "Ibu," "Ibu Putu" at the final celebration

Yaya and Tesna's son, Cok Raja

References

The majority of references are from the final papers of students—each of whom generously allowed me to share excerpts.

1. Mary Catherine Bateson. *Peripheral Vision: Learning along the Way*. HarperCollins, 1994, p. 73.
2. Fiona Reinhold
3. Shannon Esrich
4. Julia Petras
5. Julia Petras
6. Wade Davis. *The Serpent and the Rainbow: A Harvard Scientist's Astonishing Journey into the Secret Societies of Haitian Voodoo, Zombis, and Magic.* Simon & Schuster, 1985.
7. Jennifer Hawley
8. Michaela Cook
9. Jessica Estes
10. Morgan Milhomens
11. Sam Ryea
12. Michelle Bourgeois
13. Siri Rooney
14. Abby Clifford
15. Connie Coleman

16. Briana Martin
17. Paige Brandman
18. Briana Martin
19. Morgan Milhomens
20. Lexi Gadwar
21. Jayna Chelm
22. Siri Rooney
23. Carly Clark
24. Michelle Bourgeois
25. Jess Terrien
26. Carly Clark
27. Olivia Jenkins
28. Julia Petras
29. Bhumika Patel
30. Fiona Reinhold
31. Morgan Milhomens
32. Julia Petras
33. Olivia Jenkins
34. Victoria Woods
35. Connie Coleman
36. Jessica Estes
37. Connie Coleman
38. Ben Lane
39. Paige Brandman
40. Andrea Decoster
41. Olivia Jenkins
42. Luh Ketut Suriyani & Gordon Jensen. *The Balinese People: A Reinvestigation of Character.* Oxford University Press, 1992, p.47.
43. Homer Johnsen
44. Devin Russell
45. Leah Murdock
46. Devin Russell

Acknowledgments

I would especially like to express my gratitude to these people:

My superb writing mentor, Antonia Messuri, who walked with me every step of the way—challenging, supporting, and never letting me off the hook. It was a magnificent ride and I am deeply appreciative;

My readers Sandra Pascuzzi and Fiona Clancey, whose thoughtful attention to my writing confirmed my desire to share the story;

My proofreader, Nicky McLean;

And, my copyeditor and book layout and design person, Vally M. Sharpe, whose skill and creativity continually amazed me as did her deep respect for writers and their work.

About the Author

Carla Osgood grew up in Indiana farm country and the Mississippi Delta. In the mid-1960s, she entered the Peace Corps, made her home in Guyana, South America, and met David, whom she later married there.

As she describes in *Embracing Difference in a Culture of Kindness*, she and her husband have traveled to Bali, Indonesia for over two decades, using their skills as clinical psychologists to introduce university students and other professionals to the challenges of meeting cultural differences and the power of presence.

She and her husband hope to return to Bali next year. This is her first memoir.

To Purchase Additional Copies:

Embracing Difference in a Culture of Kindness
is available from Amazon.com and fine booksellers
worldwide. Also available as a Kindle eBook.

To contact the author:

email her at
carla.osgood@gmail.com

Made in the USA
Columbia, SC
19 September 2024

42626547R00089